General editor: Graham Handley MA Ph.D.

Brodie's Notes on Christopher Marlowe's
Doctor Faustus

W. S. Bunnell MA FCP

D1390219

150th YEAR
M
MACMILLAN

First published 1978 by Pan Books Ltd

This revised edition published 1993 by
THE MACMILLAN PRESS LTD
Houndmills, Basingstoke, Hampshire RG21 2XS
and London
Companies and representatives
throughout the world

ISBN 0–333–58149–0

Typeset by Footnote Graphics, Warminster, Wiltshire
Printed in Great Britain by
Cox & Wyman Ltd, Reading

Contents

A close reading of the set book is the student's primary task. These Notes will help to increase your understanding and appreciation of the play, and to stimulate *your own* thinking about it: *they are in no way intended as a substitute* for a thorough knowledge of the play.

Preface

The intention throughout this study aid is to stimulate and guide, to encourage your involvement in the book, and to develop informed responses and a sure understanding of the main details.

Brodie's Notes provide a clear outline of the play or novel's plot, followed by act, scene, or chapter summaries and/or commentaries. These are designed to emphasize the most important literary and factual details. Poems, stories or non-fiction texts combine brief summary with critical commentary on individual aspects or common features of the genre being examined. Textual notes define what is difficult or obscure and emphasize literary qualities. Revision questions are set at appropriate points to test your ability to appreciate the prescribed book and to write accurately and relevantly about it.

In addition, each of these Notes includes a critical appreciation of the author's art. This covers such major elements as characterization, style, structure, setting and themes. Poems are examined technically – rhyme, rhythm, for instance. In fact, any important aspect of the prescribed work will be evaluated. The aim is to send you back to the text you are studying.

Each study aid concludes with a series of general questions which require a detailed knowledge of the book: some of these questions may invite comparison with other books, some will be suitable for coursework exercises, and some could be adapted to work you are doing on another book or books. Each study aid has been adapted to meet the needs of the current examination requirements. They provide a basic, individual and imaginative response to the work being studied, and it is hoped that they will stimulate you to acquire disciplined reading habits and critical fluency.

Graham Handley 1990

The author and his work

Little is known definitely about the life of Christopher Marlowe. This is not unusual. We know very little about any of the great Elizabethan dramatists; even of Shakespeare, who wrote more, lived longer and was better known than Marlowe, there is hardly any significant biographical knowledge. A man needed to be aristocratic and famous in several spheres for contemporaries to take an interest in his life story, and Marlowe lacked the high birth and many-sided fame of a Sir Philip Sidney or a Sir Walter Raleigh.

Christopher Marlowe was born on 6 February 1564, the son of a Canterbury shoemaker; his mother was the daughter of a clergyman. In the year of his son's birth John Marlowe (whose name was normally spelt Marley or Marlyn) was made a Freeman of the City of Canterbury, which indicates he was a man of some standing and substance. Christopher was baptized in the church of St George in Canterbury. He was the only son, and the predominant influences in his upbringing were feminine.

He attended the King's School, Canterbury and from there went on to Bene't College, Cambridge (now known as Corpus Christi) on a six-year scholarship. His education both at school and at university was classical. He proceeded from the early study of the Latin Grammar of William Lily, the High Master of St Paul's School, to a study of Latin authors of history, drama and poetry, of Caesar and Livy, Terence and Plautus, Ovid, Vergil and Horace. At university he studied rhetoric, logic and philosophy. There was much Latin and less Greek. The importance of his education to an intellectual writer like Marlowe cannot be overestimated. We know nothing of his attitude to education, but it is unlikely that he went 'unwillingly to school' as Shakespeare perhaps did. The knowledge of the classical world plainly inspired him and excited his imagination. He went up to Cambridge in 1580 and remained there until 1587. He took his bachelor's degree in 1583–4 and his master's degree in 1587.

Marlowe may have met Francis Kett, a Fellow of Bene't College who was burned for heresy in 1589, and who may have been an influence in the shaping of Marlowe's religious opinions. There were doubtless other influences. He may later have been connected with Sir Walter Raleigh's 'school of atheism' or 'school of night': a gathering of men who prided themselves on their independence of thought. They were accused of atheism, and perhaps Marlowe's own duality of approach to religious belief, which plays a significant part in his *Doctor Faustus*, can be seen also in Raleigh. It is difficult to believe that the man who could write in his epitaph, 'But from this earth, this grave, this dust,/My God shall raise me up, I trust' was a convinced or consistent atheist.

During 1587 Marlowe was absent from university for a long period, and his Master's degree was awarded after the intervention of the Privy Council, who stated that 'he had done her Majesty good service'. He may have been sent to Rheims as a spy to report what was happening among disaffected English students in the university there.

From 1587–93 Marlowe was in London, though there is a possibility that for a time he served as a soldier in the Low Countries, as did his fellow dramatist Ben Jonson. His knowledge of military terms may be a result of this experience, but it is scarcely proof of it.

He had begun to write at Cambridge. His lively and sensuous translation of Ovid's *Amores* was certainly started there, as was perhaps the early part of *Tamburlaine*. This was his first play, which made its initial stage appearance in 1587 or 1588; it was printed in 1590. With the force of its style, its imaginative sweep and its tremendous vitality, *Tamburlaine* immediately established Marlowe as a popular dramatist. Alleyn, one of the leading actors of the day, created the role of *Tamburlaine*. Its success can be gauged not only by the number of its performances but also by the attacks of his rivals. *Tamburlaine* represented a substantial advance in the development of the English drama, explosively introducing the beginning of the great age of writing for the theatre.

The Tragical History of Doctor Faustus appeared soon after *Tamburlaine*, and was probably written and produced in 1588. His next play was *The Jew of Malta*. The first two acts are powerful and successful; the later parts show a significant decline in technique, though Marlowe's energy still breaks fitfully through. *The Troublesome Raigne and Lamentable Death of Edward the Second*, probably acted in 1592 and printed in 1593, represented a change from tragedy to history. It has been favourably compared to Shakespeare's *Richard II*. Marlowe shows real dramatic skill in ordering his material.

Like all his characters, Edward is not ennobled by suffering, yet there is a power revealed throughout this play that is noticeably absent from the earlier works.

Marlowe's two final plays – *The Massacre at Paris* and *The Tragedie of Dido, Queene of Carthage*, both produced in 1593 – do not maintain the maturing of his dramatic art shown in *Edward II*. These two final plays may have been the result of collaboration with other dramatists; Thomas Nashe (1567–1601) is named on the title-page of *Dido*.

Marlowe's hand may also be seen in his contributions to plays by other dramatists; some of the early plays of Shakespeare, such as *Titus Andronicus* and the three parts of *Henry VI*, have been mentioned in this connection.

The translation of Ovid's *Amores* was published in 1597, after Marlowe's death. *Hero and Leander*, printed in 1598, was praised by Jonson. As a poet Marlowe will be remembered for one short, exquisite lyric: 'The Passionate Shepherd to His Love', one of the most perfect poems in the English language. This was first printed in full in *England's Helicon* (1600).

While he was writing his plays it is possible that Marlowe also acted as a secret agent for Sir Francis Walsingham. He was acquainted with the Walsingham family, with Sir Walter Raleigh, possibly with the Earl of Oxford (also a poet), with mathematicians, at least one astronomer, and, of course, with his fellow writers. He was referred to by Shakespeare in *As You Like It*:

Dead Shepherd, now I find thy saw of might:
Who ever lov'd that lov'd not at first sight?

The dramatist Robert Greene (1558–92) called him 'thou famous gracer of Tragedians'; the dramatist and poet George Peele (approx. 1558–97) described him as 'the Muses' darling for thy verse', while the poet Michael Drayton (1563–1631) wrote of him:

Next Marlowe bathed in the Thespian springs
Had in him those brave translunary things
That the first Poets had, his raptures were
All ayre and fire, which made his verses cleere.

Marlowe's character was plainly rash and impatient: he was often in trouble. In 1589 he was arrested and imprisoned in Newgate for thirteen days, after a fight in which the actor

William Bradley was killed. At the trial he received a pardon for his part in this. In 1592 he was arrested for constant breaches of the peace. There were many rumours about his atheism and his homosexuality. The informer Richard Baines accused Marlowe of saying that Christ was a bastard and a homosexual. In 1593 serious charges were brought against him. Thomas Kyd, with whom Marlowe shared a room, was arrested and, after being tortured on the rack, stated that Marlowe was the owner of certain papers on atheism that had been found in their room. Marlowe was then brought before the Privy Council but released on probation. Before the charges could be further investigated, Marlowe was dead.

There are several versions of Marlowe's death. According to the contemporary writer Francis Meres (1565–1647), 'Christopher Marlowe was stabbed to death by a bawdy serving man, a rivall of his in his lewde love'. William Vaughan saw in his death 'the effects of God's justice', and described how Marlowe tried to stab one of his companions named Ingram, with whom he was feasting and gambling in a tavern in Deptford. Ingram in self-defence stabbed Marlowe in the eye 'in such sort, that his braynes coming out at the dagger's point, he shortly after died'. Thomas Beard described how, in the struggle, Marlowe stabbed his own dagger into his head. He 'cursed and blasphemed to his last gaspe, and together with his breath an oath flew out of his mouth that it was not only a manifest sign of God's Judgment, but also an horrible and fearful terror to all that beheld him.'

In *The Death of Christopher Marlowe*, Dr Leslie Hotson has established that Marlowe was killed by Ingram Frizer at an inn in Deptford on 30 May 1593. Also there were Robert Paley and Nicholas Skerres. During a quarrel about the payment of the bill Marlowe lost his temper and attacked Frizer from behind; in the struggle Marlowe was stabbed in the eye and died immediately. Frizer was later pardoned on the grounds that he had acted in self-defence. Both men were connected with the Walsinghams; possibly it was a meeting of government agents.

Marlowe's theatre

The Elizabethan dramatist

Marlowe occupies an important place in the history of the Elizabethan theatre. His four great tragedies were written between 1587 and 1593. The Globe Playhouse, the most famous of the Elizabethan theatres, was not built until 1599. An understanding of the contemporary theatre is vital to the appreciation of *Doctor Faustus*, as indeed it is for any play of any period.

The primary purpose of a dramatist is to entertain his audience. The Elizabethan audience was drawn from a variety of different backgrounds. It was an age when class distinctions were accepted as the natural order of things. Because of this acceptance there was no problem in the mingling of the different classes in the theatre. London then, as now, was the centre of dramatic activity. The court circle established the standard of taste in the theatre at one end, the common people demanded knockabout farce at the other. The two standards were not exclusive. In an age when news was circulated in the form of ballads, an enthusiasm for poetry was common to all classes. The many-sided nature of the audience may help to explain the shifts from exquisite and imaginative poetry to the coarse and sometimes brutal farce which is one of the marks of *Doctor Faustus*; a dramatist who was concerned with capturing the attention of his audience had to satisfy both appetites. It was not necessary for the comic element to be crude and obvious – the rich humour springing from the well-conceived and effectively drawn character of a Falstaff was certainly appreciated.

It was an age when the emphasis was on the spoken word. All sections of the audience – from the well-to-do sitting in the gallery to the 'groundlings' standing in front of the stage – were able to listen intently and for long periods. Although some members of the audience were illiterate, others (through the classical education they had received at the many grammar schools, and the habit of both listening to and reading English translations of the Bible), would be able easily to appreciate biblical and classical references.

Plays were performed in inn yards with their galleries, in

halls and at Court and other great houses. The inn yard represented the pattern of the Elizabethan theatre. The stage was built in the shape of an apron and thrust right into the audience. The performances took place during the day. The front part of the stage was in the open air. There was no scenery, so the setting had to be suggested by the dramatist, helped out by the simplest and most easily movable props. This meant that scene changes would present the minimum of problems. The scenes existed only in the imagination of the audience; the change of scene to Rome via a European tour was managed without difficulty in *Doctor Faustus*. The Elizabethan dramatist possessed the novelist's freedom in being able to take the whole world as his scene.

There was no attempt at naturalism in this theatre; its approach was imaginative, and its emotion and actions tended to be larger than life. The acting was vigorous and expressive. Marlowe's theatre was still very close in time and memory to the crude style of acting of the miracle and morality plays. Yet by this time the rhetorical speaking of verse had developed into an art that demanded an apprenticeship to the stage in which the control of the body, the features and the voice could be learnt. It was the business of the actor to exploit all the emotional intensity of which his lines were capable.

Shakespeare describes this 'method':

Is it not monstrous that this player here,
But in a fiction, in a dream of passion,
Could force his soul so to his own conceit
That from her working all his visage warmed;
Tears in his eyes, distraction in's aspect,
A broken voice, and his whole function suiting
With forms to his conceit?

Not surprisingly, this rhetorical method was sometimes over-done; Hamlet is offended 'to the soul to hear a robustious periwig-pated fellow tear a passion to tatters, to very rags, to split the ears of the groundlings, who for the most part are capable of nothing but inexplicable dumb shows and noise'. The actor was not separated from his audience; the apron stage enabled him to remain close, yet it also made of acting a public performance, which is not possible in the conventional picture-frame stage of today, though there have been a number of experiments in theatre of the round.

Colour was provided by the magnificence of costumes and the introduction of pageantry into court scenes. There was an abundance of movement both on the stage and in entrances and exits. The actors were grouped into companies, a statute of 1572 having proclaimed them rogues and vagabonds. They became, therefore, part of the household of important noblemen; this protected them from the operation of the law. The relationship between the dramatist and the companies was close; he would be aware of the qualities of the actors in the company for whom his play was written. It has been conjectured that *Doctor Faustus* belonged to the Earl of Pembroke's Men, by whom it was acted at court and in the theatre. The earliest recorded performance is one by the Lord Admiral's Men. Edward Alleyn, who, together with the Burbages, was one of the most famous and successful of Elizabethan actors, probably played Faustus.

Women were not allowed on the stage, and female parts were taken by boys who, according to contemporary reports, were in no way inferior to actresses. This, in part, explains the emphasis on male characters in *Doctor Faustus*. It means also that the beauty of Helen must be conveyed, by word and image, in a poetic appeal to the imagination.

The limitations of the Elizabethan stage did not represent a constraint on the dramatist: he was able to exploit the freedom, the need for poetry and imagination, and the opportunity to explore a theme in depth. From this stage emerged drama of a strength, variety and achievement that has never been equalled at any time or in any country.

The text, history and influence of the play

The text of most Elizabethan plays presents a problem. Primarily they were written for the theatre and were part of the assets of the company that owned them. It was against the interest of the company to print the play until the first run of performances was over or until 'pirated' editions had appeared. The text of *Doctor Faustus* presents a bigger problem than usual, even for Elizabethan plays. The confusion is largely caused by the substantial additions that were made to the play. There are two texts of major importance in the printings of *Dr Faustus*. The first, commonly known as the A text, was published in 1604 while the second, known as the B text, appeared in 1616. The B version is more than one third as long again as the A version, though some of the material is thought not to have been written by Marlowe.

At the time when this Brodie Note was first written, the preference was for the A text, but in order to give as full a version of the play as possible, the notes here refer mainly to the edition (the B text) published in 1616. The modern edition used for these notes is that edited by John D. Jump, first published in 1965, reprinted many times (last in 1988) and thus a reliable text for the present-day student to use. It is published by Routledge.

The most commonly accepted date for the writing and production of *Doctor Faustus* is 1588. This date, however, has been disputed.

The source of the story of Doctor Faustus, who lived from about 1500 to 1545, is a German work published in Frankfurt in 1587, the *Historia von D. Iohan Faustus*. This story, like that of Don Juan, was destined to become one of the great myths of the western world. The purpose of the story was moral; and its spirit is that of the protestant reformation, with a strong feeling against the papacy. The German work was soon translated and published in England. The earliest surviving edition of this is dated 1592, and its title was *The Historie of the damnable life and deserued death of Doctor Iohn Faustus*. There were doubtless other translations before this and it must have been one of these that Marlowe used. There is, however, no record of such a work; the surviving edition uses the words 'Newly imprinted' on its title-page, and this suggests that an earlier version had previously been printed. The evidence of the source of the play would point to a date of composition later than 1588. Indeed it would favour 1592–3, which would make *Doctor Faustus* Marlowe's final play. This later dating would also remove the problem of placing a play with a mature and developed style within a year or two of the immature *Tamburlaine*.

A *Ballad of the life and deathe of Doctor Faustus, the great Cunjerer* was licensed in February 1589. There is a strong likelihood, but no certainty, that this could have been inspired by the popularity of the translation of the *Life*, or by Marlowe's play.

There are two historical references in the play which, if they are topical, would favour the earlier date. One of these references is to the Duke of Parma, who was governor-general of the Low Countries from 1579 to 1592. In 1588 the Spanish

Armada, under the command of the Duke of Parma, made its attempt to invade England. English interest in the Duke would have been at its height around 1588. The other reference is to 'the fiery keel at Antwerp's bridge', which took place in April 1585. This incident would certainly have faded from popular consciousness by 1592–3. Neither of these references conclusively supports an earlier date.

All we can be certain about is that *Doctor Faustus* was written and produced at some time between 1588 and 1593.

The play was probably first *published* in 1601, eight years after Marlowe's death. The earliest existing edition is a quarto, *The Tragical History of D. Faustus*. As it hath been Acted by the Right Honorable the Earle of Nottingham his servants. Written by Ch. Marlowe. London. Printed by V.S. for Thomas Bushell. 1604.'

Various names have been suggested as collaborators in the play – Dekker, Nashe and Rowley – but the purist will want to see Marlowe's hand only in the best of it. There is, however, no reason to suppose that Marlowe, a working dramatist who was almost certainly dependent upon the theatre for his living, was unwilling to give the audience what it wanted; he included humour as well as high tragedy. From the general nature of Marlowe's work, it is clear that his mind was serious and intellectual rather than humorous. His was not the kind of mind that would be interested in the quirks and oddities of human character, nor did he live long enough to develop such an interest anyway. There is, then, no reason why, when he turned to humour, he should not descend to all the obvious devices of knockabout farce. Certainly the play needed a middle part; whether this was provided by Marlowe or other hands, it remains a part of the play as we have it.

The great and serious scenes in verse at the beginning and the end are by Marlowe. The tendency of the modern editor is to attempt to harmonize the two texts while perhaps leaning more heavily on the later. The aim should be to produce a text which ensures that the tragedy is not overwhelmed by the farce and that the comic scenes remain, in Elizabethan terms, an organic part of the play. This means generally that they should include the character Faustus, and that they should be a comment on the main, serious theme of the play.

Since Marlowe's time, the theme and his play have proved to be of enduring interest. The best-known and the greatest representation of the theme is by the German poet Goethe.

His play is in two parts: in the first, the relationship between Faust and Gretchen is important. There is a sustained poetic approach, and the human aspects are emphasized far more strongly than in *Doctor Faustus*. The second part, which took Goethe over forty years to write, traces the progress of Faust to ultimate salvation. German writers who have dealt with the theme include Lessing, Weidmann, Muller, Klinger, and, more recently, the novelist Thomas Mann in his *Doktor Faustus*.

Dorothy Sayers, the writer of the Lord Peter Wimsey detective novels, wrote a play on the theme, *The Devil to Pay* (1939), which keeps broadly to Marlowe's version, though the approach is more sophisticated.

In music, the theme has inspired Boito's opera *Mefistofele* (1866), Gounod's ever-popular *Faust* (1859), Berlioz's *La Damnation de Faust* (1893) and Busoni's *Doktor Faust* (1925).

Doctor Faustus was performed in the later part of the seventeenth century, after the reopening of the theatres at the restoration of the monarchy. During the present century it has often been revived, not only in England but also in Germany and America. It has been broadcast, televised and filmed.

Plot and summary

Marlowe, like Shakespeare and other contemporary dramatists, cared little about the originality of their plots. The play was fundamentally a medium for the telling of a story. In the chronicle type of play – and that essentially is what *Doctor Faustus* is – there is no attempt to keep to unities of time, place or action. Indeed, the whole concept of the 'dramatic unities' (e.g. limiting the timing of a play to the time taken to act it, or to a single day) was completely foreign to the nature of Elizabethan drama. Of course, dramatists of the stature of Marlowe and Shakespeare personalized their sources in terms of character and transferred the spirit of the narrative by the force and greatness of their imagination. Nevertheless, the source remains an important element in the consideration of the plot.

Marlowe's source here is *The Historie of the damnable life and deserued death of Doctor Iohn Faustus*, written in German and translated into English. The outline and much of the detail of the story dominate the play; there is very little actual invention of incident by Marlowe. In turning a prose narrative into dramatic form there is a great deal of movement of emphasis and compression.

Faustus himself in *The Historie* is viewed objectively. As the title implies, the moral purpose in narrative terms looms very large. Marlowe's study of the personality of Faustus is much more subjective. As Havelock Ellis points out, Faust is, in Marlowe's version, no mere magician, but the portrait of a real man, another type of Tamburlaine, thirsting not for earthly dominion but for infinity; the sinner of the narrative has become the hero of the drama. Marlowe obviously found the theme congenial and one which mirrored closely his own intellectual preoccupations and emotional state.

Doctor Faustus is in no sense autobiographical except insofar as all genuine art springs from the experiences and emotions of the artist. Yet one of the faults of the play is that it tends to be too subjective a work; it lacks warm humanity in its general approach. Marlowe never breaks the bounds of his own egotistical intellectuality, his fierce inward rather than outward-turning imagination, and the simplicity of the conflict between sin and damnation. He fails to reconcile the full life with redemption. The extension of the limits of experience can be good and fulfilling as well as sinful and negative. This is Marlowe's dilemma; he is caught between his source and his own subjective preoccupation. Given greater maturity and dramatic experience Marlowe might have been able to resolve these conflicts, but we have to remember that *Doctor Faustus* is the production of a young man – whether we regard it as his second play or one written towards the end of his life. Marlowe made a tremendous advance over his predecessors in ordering his dramatic material; in none of his plays did he achieve complete success in this. *Doctor Faustus* remains a collection of dramatic scenes rather than a drama, and the achievement in individual scenes ranges from the crude to the magnificent.

Marlowe was still very close to the period of miracle (a play based on biblical subjects or episodical scenes from the life of a saint, usually produced in cycles) and morality plays. As the title implies, these were plays with a definite moral purpose, often narrowly didactic and dull, sermons in dramatic form. *Doctor Faustus* has been called an inverted morality play, where the controlling impulse is towards evil rather than good. The final speech of the Chorus may be in conflict with much in the play, but its feeling is close to that of the morality play.

From the morality play comes the element of allegory in *Doctor Faustus*, the Good and Evil Angels and the Old Man; the theme of the struggle between vice and virtue for the possession of the soul of man. In spite of their moral purpose, the 'moralities' sometimes contained a great amount of crudity; and the level of clowning was closely related to that in the comic scenes of *Doctor Faustus*.

Modern audiences have the problem of accepting the supernatural. Dorothy Sayers writes in the Preface to *The Devil to Pay*:

In whatever way we retell the tale of Faustus, the supernatural element *is* the story. For the 'two-hours traffic of our stage', we must indulge in the 'willing suspension of disbelief'. We must accept magic and miracle as physical realities; we must admit the possibility of genuine witchcraft, of the strange legal transaction by which a man might sell his soul to Satan, of the actual appearance of the Devil in concrete bodily shape. The Faustus legend is dyed in grain with the thought and feeling of its period.

One error we must not make is to assume that Marlowe shared our doubts. Renaissance man and freethinker he may have been, but no man of that time could throw off completely the strong belief in superstition he had inherited from centuries of acceptance and fear of it. The test dramatically is whether we can accept the framework of sin and damnation and whether the dramatist presents them to us convincingly enough to compel our belief. Marlowe does, and indeed the task is not so difficult as the 20th-century man commonly assumes. We are still far from free from the superstition and dogma that the medieval mind accepted without question.

It is easier to control a theme leading to resolution and light than one leading to darkness; it is happier to identify with a hero whose suffering will lead to salvation and enlightenment. Hamlet and Lear are more sympathetic heroes than Macbeth – and Faustus's case is worse than his. This has led some critics to speculate on whether Marlowe could have 'saved' Faustus. Such speculation is academic, for no dramatist at that time would have been likely to make such a fundamental change in his handling of the source material; it would also have destroyed much of the force and meaning of the play. Part of the development lies in the realization in the mind of Faustus that he is actually to be eternally damned. This is a logical conclusion to the frivolous and vainglorious way in which he approaches the initial compact – he has to learn that hell is no fable. As the sardonic Mephistophilis (spelt 'Mephostophilis' in the B text) comments, 'Ay, think so still, till experience change thy mind'. It is this final knowledge that gives real unity to the plot, from the refusal to believe in hell to:

Let Faustus live in hell a thousand years,
A hundred thousand and at last be sav'd.
O, no end is limited to damned souls.

One of the continuing conflicts in the play is whether Faustus will repent, and this interest is kept alive and in the mind of the audience almost to the end. It must be assumed that, on one level, the contract is not binding and that Christ's blood and mercy can lead to forgiveness for any man. On another level, it can be argued that to make a formal compact is to show a strong disposition to evil – that is, unbelief. Goethe's *Faust*, at the end of Part II, achieved salvation, but that is a work very different in feeling and philosophy from Marlowe's. The wheel comes full circle to Faustus in many ways, and again in terms of plot gives a fine balance to the play. Faustus, who wanted to be more than man, who desired the power and knowledge of a god, finally begs to be less than man:

and I be chang'd
Unto some brutish beast! all beasts are happy,
For, when they die,
Their souls are soon dissolv'd in elements.

The unity of the play lies in two moments: the selling of Faustus's soul to the devil, and the final rendering up of that soul. Both these moments are magnificently presented and dramatically expressed.

The problem is the twenty-four years that Faustus gains. Older critics harshly condemned Marlowe's handling of this problem. Francis Jeffrey spoke of 'disgusting buffoonery and low farce'. Hazlitt spoke of those scenes in which Faustus was not directly concerned as, 'mean and grovelling to the last degree'. When Goethe exclaimed of Marlowe's play, 'How greatly it is all planned!' it is assumed he was thinking only of the overall conception and the balance between the first and last parts of the play. Marlowe (and his collaborators, or those who later added material) had a very difficult task to overcome – one that no serious attempt was made to solve. The passage of time was represented by a series of single incidents, largely unrelated to each other and to the main theme. In one sense these incidents are dramatically important: they gave the audience of Marlowe's day the comedy they demanded.

Doctor Faustus, in this duality between a high moral theme and knockabout farce, is in the direct tradition of the morality play. The nature of these scenes in terms of the impact of our conception of Faustus's character should not worry us too much. His use of his powers is not noble and dignified. But this is the logic of his initial act and his submission to evil: evil begets evil. Hedonism may be a pleasant pursuit but it is not one usually characterized by nobility and dignity. The real pathos of these scenes is that Faustus is there not for what he is, but for what he can do. The magician has overwhelmed the man: even his magic power springs not from himself but from Mephostophilis, for it is he who makes Alexander and his lady appear, and he who fetches the grapes for the duchess.

There is some attempt to relate these episodes to the main plot. Wagner uses his master's language, and in doing so mocks scholastic philosophy. The stealing of the Pope's dish is matched by the stealing of the vintner's goblet. Mephostophilis could be described as a link man between the two levels. Compared, however, with the close linking and balancing of themes in later plays, these connections are spasmodic and ineffective. We cannot begin to speak of main plot and subplot.

The matter is one of degree. The basic plan of the play lies between the two points of the compact and the final dramatization, together with the passage of twenty-four years:

So he will spare him four-and-twenty years,
Letting him live in all voluptuousness
Having thee ever to attend on me,
To give me whatsoever I shall ask,
To tell me whatsoever I demand,
To slay mine enemies and aid my friends,
And always be obedient to my will.

The middle part is acceptable so long as it does not dominate the impression left in the mind of the audience by the end and the beginning. Without the middle part there would be no play either in length or in dramatic movement, comedy, spectacle or the representation of life.

Either way, they are a part of the play. We are left with a work which, in construction, moves between strength and weakness, from close logical unity to the episodic, and which combines sublime tragedy with the crudest farce.

Scene summaries, critical commentary, textual notes and revision questions

Chorus

The Chorus sets the scene, introduces the story and tells the audience something of Faustus and his background. Faustus was born of lowly parents in a town called Rhode in Germany. At the Wittenberg university he excelled in his studies in divinity and became a doctor. His pride in his learning led to forbidden studies in magic; his delight in magic he placed before his salvation.

Already in the language of the chorus an ironic note is being sounded. The inflated heroic language acts as a counterpoint to the themes of the play, which are the reverse of heroic. The phrase 'good or bad' indicates the nature of the irony, and this is further underlined by the fact that the plot is spelled out and yet it does not diminish our interest in the forthcoming action. Note the particularly evocative language used to indicate the nature of Faustus's predictions – 'swollen', 'glutted', 'surfeits', 'chiefest bliss'.

Trasimene A lake in Italy where Hannibal defeated the Romans in 217 BC.
Mars The Roman God of War.
mate Support.
Carthagens Carthaginians led by Hannibal. These lines suggest Marlowe's own change of scene from *Tamburlaine* to this play.
state Power, government.
muse Poet.
vaunt Boast of.
Rhode Now Stadtrode.
Wittenberg (Wertenberg in the 1604 Quarto). A town in Saxony, the seat of a famous university. It was, through Luther, closely connected with the establishment of German Protestantism.
Whereas Where.
scholarism The learning of the 'schools'.
grac'd with doctor's name Granted the degree of doctor.
sweetly Effectively; perhaps also the idea that it is done so well that its excellence gives pleasure.
cunning knowledge.
waxen wings This is a reference to the story of Icarus who flew

with his father from Crete. The sun melted the wax fastening his
wings and he fell into the sea.

necromancy Predicting the future by calling up the spirits of the
dead.

chiefest bliss The salvation of his soul.

Scene 1

When the play opens Faustus is seated in his study at a table
with his books around him. He soliloquizes on the different
branches of learning, dismissing logic, economy, medicine,
law and divinity. He turns to the books of magic, which
promise power and joy. The magician has powers which make
him godlike. Wagner enters and Faustus asks him to request
Valdes and Cornelius to visit him. The Good and Evil Angels
enter. The Good Angel warns Faustus of the dangers of the
book of magic. The Evil Angel tempts him with the promise of
knowledge and the power assured by magic to those who
follow it. Faustus's imagination leaps to develop the possibilities held out by the Evil Angel.

When Valdes and Cornelius enter, Faustus tells them that
he has utterly surrendered to the delights of magic, and seeks
their help. Valdes and Cornelius, like the Evil Angel, expound
the miraculous power of magic, and Faustus demands a de-
monstration. They undertake to instruct Faustus in the arts of
magic. After dinner Faustus swears he will try to conjure, even
if death be the penalty.

Faustus, like Marlowe, is a man of his time, a Renaissance
man excited by the thought of the powers which magic knowledge will confer upon him, and his language reflects this. The
blank verse employs exaggerated images and rhetorical questions. Note the strong 'e', 'p' and 't' sounds, which suggest by
these sounds the extremes to which Faustus will go. There is a
sense of movement, too, the 'searching' images, questing for
treasure and sensory satisfaction, reflect both the Elizabethan
love of adventure and exploration and Faustus's own frame of
mind. They thus form a microcosmic mirror-image of man
and time. As the scene progresses we see Faustus being swept
along, the metaphysical language enhanced by classical and
topical allusions which give it a rare density of association.
Tension rises as he moves towards his fatal decision. The
dramatic climax, 'This night I'll conjure, though I die' is full
of irony. Notice also the irony of Cornelius's question – 'what
shall we three want' – describing Faustus and his companions

as an unholy Trinity. We shall see later in Scene 3 that Faustus is to reject the concept of the Holy Trinity. The Good and Bad Angels are crucial to the structure of the play, defining the balance of decision and indecision which plagues Faustus and which provides so much dramatic continuity to the play. They derive as personifications from the earlier morality plays, and show Marlowe adapting the tradition he knows so well. Their four-line speeches are virtually incantations to good and evil. The contrasting use of verse in this scene is also an index to the two sides of Faustus's soliloquy. To be prepared to play God you have to reject God, and the blank verse rhetoric of Faustus shows him going beyond spiritual confines and embracing the delicious possibility of supreme power – which in his case will ironically carry its own confines.

commenc'd Graduated, here as a doctor.

Aristotle The great Greek philosopher (384–322 BC), a pupil of Plato. He influenced thinking in philosophy, logic, science and literature. Latin versions of his work had a profound influence on medieval thought. *Analytics* is the title of one of his works.

Bene disserere . . . logices (Latin). This is translated in the next line of the text.

wit Mind.

on kae me (Greek). Being and not being.

Galen Galenus Claudius (*c.* AD 129–199), wrote many treatises on medicine. As Aristotle dominated philosophy so Galen dominated medical thinking in the Middle Ages.

ubi desinit . . . medicus (Latin). Where the philosopher breaks off, here the doctor begins.

Summum bonum medicinae sanitas (Latin). Loosely translated on the next line. More accurately it means, 'The greatest good of medicine is health.' The phrase is taken from Aristotle.

aphorisms From the *Aphorisms* of Hippocrates, the 'father' of medicine. Here it means, 'hints on principles of medicine'.

bills Prescriptions.

Justinian Justinian I (AD 527–65) was the emperor of Constantinople. He was famous for the code of law associated with his name.

Si una . . . rei (Latin). If one and the same thing is left to two people, the one shall have the object, the other its value.

Exhereditare . . . nisi (Latin). A father cannot disinherit his son, unless . . .

Institute *The Institutes* were intended as an introduction to the subsequent work on Roman Law.

Jerome's Bible St Jerome (*c* AD 340–420), after a time of dissipation became a hermit. He was responsible for the Latin translation of the Bible, known as the Vulgate.

Stipendium peccati mors est This is immediately translated as in the text, as is the next Latin sentence from St John, 1, 8.

Che sarà, sarà (Italian). The translation immediately follows this in the text.

metaphysics Supernatural philosophy.

Lines . . . characters The stock-in-trade of the magician.

artisan One instructed in an art.

exceeds Excels.

conference Conversation.

damned book Of magic.

Jove This is a poetical name for Jupiter, the chief god of the Romans. Here Jove is used for God in the Christian concept.

elements Earth, water, fire and air.

conceit Imagination of the power referred to in the previous lines.

Resolve . . . ambiguities Clear up all doubts of meaning.

new-found world A reference to the voyages of exploration, America.

delicates Delicacies.

Rhine Wittenberg is situated on the River Elbe, not the Rhine.

Prince of Parma Governor-general of the Low Countries. He was the leader of the Spanish forces that embarked in the Armada to conquer England. This is a contemporary reference.

brunt Violent attack.

fiery keel A fire-ship. This refers to an action during the siege of Antwerp where such a ship was used by the Dutch to breach the bridge over the Scheldt.

receive no object Harbour no ideas from outside, or accept no objections.

syllogisms A form of reasoning.

Gravell'd Defeated, puzzled.

Musaeus A legendary Greek poet, reputed to be the pupil of Orpheus. This is a reference to the underworld described in Virgil's *Aeneid*.

Agrippa Henricus Cornelius Agrippa (1486–1535) was a writer on magic. He was visited by famous people, including the Earl of Surrey.

shadows Spirits of the dead.

Moors The American Indians. Spain had conquered parts of South America.

Almain rutters German horsemen. (From French *Allemand* and German *Reiters*.)

Lapland The Elizabethans had strange and wonderful ideas of the peoples of the more remote parts of their world.

airy Heavenly.

queen of love Venus.

golden fleece A reference to Jason, a hero of Greek legend, who set sail in the Argo to gain the golden fleece. The reference here is to the ships carrying the gold from America to the treasury of Philip II of Spain.

object it not Do not make it an objection.

tongues Languages, especially Latin.

well seen in Having extensive knowledge of.

frequented Visited, sought after.

Delphian oracle A town at the foot of Mount Parnassus, where a temple of Apollo was situated, from which the priestess delivered an oracle (i.e. wisdom, advice, prophecy).

massy Huge.

lusty Pleasing.

Bacon Roger Bacon (1214–92) was a Franciscan monk who was in constant trouble with the Church for his opinions. He was popularly regarded as a magician.

Abanus A reference either to Pietro d'Abano (1250–1316), an Italian philosopher who was also reputed to be a magician, or to Albertus Magnus, Albert the Great (1193–1280). He was a Dominican monk, philosopher and scientist. He became Bishop of Regensburg. His experiments in science brought him under suspicion of practising the art of magic.

canvass The meaning here is 'consider, sort out'.

quiddity Minute detail, a term used in medieval scholastic philosophy.

Scene 2

Outside the house two scholars ask Wagner the whereabouts of Faustus. Wagner, in a parody of the language used in learned argument, tells them his master is dining with Valdes and Cornelius. The scholars fear for Faustus when they hear he is with two such famed practitioners of the damned magic art.

The ever-present irony is picked up in Wagner's first re-mark 'God in heaven knows', since 'his master' is on the point of losing his soul and hence his God. Note the contrast of this language with the language of the previous scene – Wagner's language is pseudo-academic and inflated, so that we have almost a parody on a comic level of the actual language already employed in unsweet reason by Faustus. It is a further irony therefore that he is able to get the verbal better of the two scholars: 'prone to lechery – to love I would say' picks up themes of temptation and rejection in the play. And in quoting 'and so the Lord bless you . . .' Wagner is ironically employing the blessing at the end of a church service. Even the repetition has an incantatory sound, and the two scholars act as important Christian or moral indicators that evil is about to triumph over Faustus. Yet they express a common fear perhaps that man cannot overcome evil, even with aid.

mobile Able to move. Wagner is imitating the language he has heard Faustus and his companions using.

like a precisian Like a Puritan. The Puritans with their solemn manner were often mocked on the stage.

Rector The Principal of the University.

sic probo (Latin). Thus I prove it.

presently Immediately.

licentiates Graduates able to proceed to a Master's or Doctor's degree.

corpus naturale (Latin). Natural body.

Scene 3

The scene is a grove, and Faustus enters to conjure spirits. He tries his magic arts, and Mephostophilis appears. Faustus tells him to return dressed like a Franciscan friar: he is wildly excited by his power over Mephostophilis, who points out, however, that he is Lucifer's servant. Mephostophilis says that he came in the hope of gaining Faustus's soul; it is Faustus's blasphemy rather than the art of conjuring that has brought him. Faustus boasts of his courage, lightly dismissing his soul and its salvation. Mephostophilis openly describes Lucifer's fall from heaven; hell is separation from the presence of God and the everlasting joys of heaven. Faustus sells his soul to Lucifer in return for twenty-four years of sensual pleasure, the services of Mephostophilis, the granting of all his demands, the answering of all his questions, the death of his enemies, the helping of his friends and the unceasing obedience of Mephostophilis. Faustus sees in Mephostophilis the attainment of all worldly power. He eagerly awaits his return.

This is the crucial early scene of the play. Again it opens with a soliloquy as Faustus determines to make magic work for him, but monologue gives way to sometimes impassioned dialogue when Mephostophilis enters. The running irony embraces the fact that Faustus thinks that he has power, but it isn't absolute. Confined by God, he is soon to be confined by the power of Lucifer. Mephostophilis is much more than a servant: he is also a voice of warning. His utterances are prophetic and celebratory of what was, as well as uncompromisingly realistic of what is – for those who are rejected by God. His pointed and poignant use of the word 'frivolous' is both warning and self-anguish, and 'Why this is hell, nor am I out of it' is definitive of his state and the coming state of Faustus. Faustus's tone is perhaps a mixture of arrogance and bravado. The spacial nature of Faustus' imagery has already been noted, and we might add that it effectively contrasts with the confined nature in time and action of his power.

Orion's drizzling look A constellation of stars, suggesting a hunter with sword at belt, most clearly seen in winter.

anagrammatiz'd Changing the order of letters to form new words.

adjunct Heavenly body.

signs The signs of the Zodiac.

erring stars Planets.

Sint mihi ... Mephostophilis (Latin). May the gods of Acheron be favourable to us! May the threefold godhead of Jehovah be favourable! Hail, spirits of fire, air, water and earth! Belzebub, prince of the east, monarch of burning hell, and Demogorgon, we propitiate you, that Mephostophilis may appear and arise! Why do you delay? By Jehova, Gehenna (hell) and the holy water which I now pour and by the sign of the cross which I now make, and by our prayers, may Mephostophilis in person now arise! In some versions Lucifer is referred to as the prince of the east and Belzebub only as a monarch of burning hell, thus making up a trinity of hell. Acheron is the regions of hell. (Belzebub is nowadays spelt 'Beelzebub'; has also been called 'Lord of the flies'.)

Franciscan friar In Protestant countries there was considerable feeling against the friars. It is an insult to represent the devil as a friar.

conjuror laureate Usually applied to a poet, the laurel was a mark of outstanding distinction.

Quin ... imagine (Latin). For in the shape of thy brother Mephostophilis, you have power.

per accidens Not the real cause.

rack Here means castigates.

confounds hell in Elysium Does not distinguish hell from heaven. Elysium is the Greek underworld where the 'old philosophers' dwell.

passionate Moved.

thorough Through.

bind Bound.

continent Joined by land.
speculation Intensive study.

Scene 4

Wagner and the Clown (Robin) enter. Wagner is trying to persuade the Clown to enter his service; he summons two devils, Baliol and Belcher, to his assistance. The Clown finally agrees to follow Wagner.

A complete contrast to the previous scene, as Marlowe gives the audience comic relief, a direct antidote to the dramatic tension raised by Faustus's expectations and evident corruption. Wagner commands the clown as Faustus has commanded his 'servant' Mephostophilis. The repartee is terse and witty. Notice the irony of 'he would give his soul to the devil, for a shoulder of mutton'. The parody element of the preceding scene is evident, and we notice that Wagner's activities do not involve the complete corruption of Faustus. Yet there is an edge to the whole scene, almost as if the parody itself is a sick joke.

pickedevants Pointed beards, then much in fashion, as can be seen from contemporary portraits.
comings in Wages.
Quo mihi discipulus (Latin). You who are my disciple, from a poem by William Lily, famed for his Latin grammar.
Stavesacre Seeds that destroy vermin. It may also be a kind of cloth corresponding with beaten (embroidered) silk. Presumably Wagner hits the Clown as he sings.
familiars Attendant and obedient devils.
guilders Dutch coins.
Banio! Belcher Invented by Wagner. Banio is 'Baliol' in some editions, or a variant used by the Clown.
diametrally (Other spellings are also used.) Diametrically.
quasi ... insistere (Latin). As if treading in our footsteps.

Scene 5

Faustus, in his study, meditates on his damnation; the Good and Evil Angels emphasize that his choice is still open. Faustus, however, is still anxious for the promised glories and power symbolized in Mephostophilis. When he returns, he demands from Faustus a formal compact with Lucifer, couched in legal terms and sealed with Faustus's blood. The blood congeals and require fire to dissolve it. Instead of writing, 'Faustus gives to thee his soul;' the inscription on his arm reads '*Homo, fuge!*' Faustus is depressed, but Mephostophilis produces a show of devils to delight his mind. The deed is then exchanged in which Faustus will yield up his soul to Lucifer in twenty-four years, and meanwhile have the services of Mephostophilis to do his bidding. He begins to question Mephostophilis about hell. He learns that, apart from heaven, hell is everywhere, it exists, and is no fable – as Faustus would like to think. Damnation, too, is real – the existence of Mephostophilis proves that. Faustus desires a wife, and for this he is reproved by Mephostophilis, who will not hear of marriage. Mephostophilis gives him a book containing lines the use of which will grant him astonishing powers.

Faustus in doubt, swaying backwards and forwards over what he has done, and the projections of the Good and the Bad Angel are dramatic equivalents to the debate in his mind, a singular and direct dramatic technique. Notice that 'Veni, veni Mephostophilis' is a parody of the invocation to the Holy Ghost, 'Veni Sancte Spiritus', which is used in Christian worship, particularly at Easter. Faustus's summons here indicates his worship of another God. Faustus's stabbing of himself has strong overtones of religious ritual, but the visual and dramatic effect shows Marlowe's deliberate craftmanship. 'Why streams it not . . . afresh' is a particularly arresting description which is reinvoked with strong Christian overtones at the end of the play. Faustus is to be a 'spirit', a word which to the Elizabethan audience would mean a devil.

signory of Emden, Lordship of this wealthy port in Prussia (Hanover).
Veni (Latin). Come.
Solamen . . . doloris (Latin). It is a comfort to the miserable to have companions in their misery. No source is known.
proper Own.
bill Deed.
set on it i.e. so that the fire will prevent the blood from congealing.
Consummatum est It is finished. These are the last words spoken by Christ on the cross, John 19, 30.
Homo fuge (Latin). Fly, O man.
On these conditions . . . wheresoever This is full of legal terminology, much of it still current.
fond Foolish.
cull Gather.
Penelope Wife of Ulysses; she ignored the importunate demands

of her suitors despite her husband's absence for twenty years.
Her story is told in Homer's *Odyssey*.

Saba The Queen of Sheba, who visited Solomon. She is referred
to in the *Koran*, 27 as Saba.

iterating Reiterating.

warrant Assure.

Revision questions, Scenes 1–5

1 Why do the known branches of knowledge fail to satisfy
Faustus?

2 Faustus is fully warned, not only by the Angels but also
by Mephostophilis himself, of the implications of what he is
doing. How far is this true?

3 Why does Faustus undertake to sell his soul?

4 Intellectual curiosity to excess is Faustus's undoing. How
far is this true?

5 The excitement of the opening of the play lies rather in
the verse than in the action. Discuss.

Scene 6

Faustus stands at the window of his study, looking up at the
sky, miserable at being deprived of the joys of heaven.
Mephostophilis tells him that man is more glorious than the
heaven that was made for him. The Good and Evil Angels
fight for and against Faustus's repentance. He despairs, as his
heart is unable to repent. Only thoughts of pleasure have
prevented his taking his own life. He questions Mephostophilis about astrology: their discussion is abruptly interrupted
when Faustus asks who made the world and Mephostophilis
refuses to answer. Faustus dismisses him harshly. The Good
and Evil Angels resume their struggle for Faustus's soul.
Lucifer, Belzebub and Mephostophilis enter. Lucifer asserts
that Faustus has no hope of salvation. Faustus vows not to
think of heaven or of God. Lucifer causes the Seven Deadly
Sins to appear, to entertain Faustus. Each in turn speaks to
Faustus – Pride, Covetousness, Wrath, Envy, Gluttony, Sloth
and Lust. Lucifer promises Faustus all kinds of delight in hell,
and promises to send for him at midnight.

Notice the effectiveness of the contradictory images of death
and those of sweet music. These and the subsequent passage
of astronomical discussion reveal the disturbed and emotional
state of Faustus's thoughts, his 'distress'd soul', and his fever-

ish questing and questioning. His apprehensions lead as ever to the appearance and interaction of the Good and Bad Angels. The manifestation of Lucifer himself shows what great store is set on the corruption of a soul – the real battle for that of Faustus is now on in deadly earnest. The pageant of the Seven Deadly Sins is diversion with a method, another effective dramatic device which peoples the stage, but before that the cut and thrust of Faustus's dialogue with the devils shows Marlowe the master of his craft – the exchanges are full of aggression with short, sharp sentences and with strong phrases of command. With the Seven Deadly Sins we descend appropriately into prose. The prose is earthy with the corruptions of human nature.

yet Still.

blind Homer Homer, the great Greek epic poet, the author of
  The Iliad and *The Odyssey*, was reputed to be blind.

Alexander's Alexander is another name for Paris, who took
  Helen to Troy and thus started the Trojan War. Oenon was
  rejected by Paris and in revenge refused to help him when he
  was dying. She died of remorse.

he, that built the walls of Thebes Amphion with the music of
  his lyre was able to move huge rocks to make the walls of
  Thebes.

centric earth The Elizabethans believed that the earth was the
  centre of the universe. The other heavenly bodies were set in
  spheres which revolved around the earth. Beyond the spheres
  was the 'empyreal orb' or 'heaven', made out of fire.

termine Terminus.

erring stars Planets.

situ et tempore (Latin). Both in place and time.

poles of the world The Axle on which all the spheres are set.

freshmen's suppositions A freshman is a university student in his
  first year; the term is still used. Hence an elementary supposition.

intelligentia Controlling spirit. Angels were thought to be
  responsible for the turning of the spheres.

coleum igneum et crystallium Fiery sphere and crystalline

conjunctions, oppositions, aspects, eclipses Different positions
  of the heavenly bodies in relation to each other.

Per ... totius (Latin). Through their unequal motion relative to
  the whole.

Move Press.

interest Here used in the legal sense.

Seven Deadly Sins These are an addition by Marlowe to the
  Faust legend. The representation of these Sins was popular in
  medieval drama and poetry. Chaucer and Langland used them.

soon Immediately.
Ovid's flea From 'Song of the Flea', a medieval poem – not by Ovid.
periwig A small wig.
arras Woven cloth ornamented with figures.
chimney-sweeper and an oyster-wife Black and smelly.
shall be May be.
bevers Food between meals, 'snacks'.
Martlemas The day when all livestock was killed and salted. Notice the alliteration in this, i.e. Peter Pickled.
March-beer Matured beer, originally brewed in March.
Lechery Sometimes given only as 'L'.

Scene 7

Robin the clown enters. He is so preoccupied with his studies in a conjuring book that he cannot attend to the horses. He promises to bring Dick all manner of delights through his conjuring powers.

The Chorus describes how Faustus has travelled through the Universe in a chariot drawn by dragons. He has now arrived in Rome to see the Pope and attend St Peter's feast.

The rustic comedians were a traditional feature of the medieval mystery plays which was continued in the Elizabethan theatre. Although *Dr Faustus* is principally a play of ideas and philosophy with demanding intellectual dialogues, Marlowe also employs vigorous action and broad comedy – varying his language appropriately, to keep the play moving and to ensure wider audience interest. In effect this is another parody sequence, a clown or low-life equivalent to Faustus's setting himself up.

The Chorus' description of Faust's journey round the universe suggests an echo of Christ's Temptation in the Wilderness, in which the devil offers Jesus all the kingdoms of the world (*Luke* 4: 5–9).

A per se 'a' by itself. This expresses his difficulty in reading the book.
deny orgon Demogorgon, one of the princes of hell.
'Snails God's nails. Contractions of oaths are a commonplace on the Elizabethan stage.
hostry Inn, tavern.
an If.
in good sadness Seriously.
muscadine Muscatel wine.

malmsey A sweet wine made in Madeira.
whippincrust Hippocras, a cordial made from wine, named after
  Hippocrates, the 'father' of medicine.
hold-belly-hold As much as you can drink, a bellyful.
Olympus' top The dwelling-place of the Greek gods.
tropics i.e. of Cancer and Capricorn.
primum mobile (Latin). The last of the spheres.

Scene 8

Faustus and Mephostophilis discuss how Faustus will spend
his four-and-twenty years of liberty. Faustus describes how in
eight days they viewed heaven, earth and hell, riding on their
dragons. Mephostophilis suggests the pranks they can play on
the Pope. The Pope, the Cardinals, the Bishops, Raymond,
King of Hungary and a chained Bruno (a Pope supported by
the Emperor in opposition to the Pope in Rome), enter. The
Pope threatens to depose the Emperor for his support of
Bruno; he is determined that Bruno shall abase himself before
the papal throne. The Cardinals leave, and Faustus commands Mephostophilis to make them sleep so that he and
Mephostophilis can assume the shape of the Cardinals, in
order to speak with the Pope, free Bruno and take him to
Germany.

Faustus and Mephostophilis enter, dressed as Cardinals.
They recommend that Bruno and the Emperor be condemned
as heretics. The Pope instructs them to take Bruno as prisoner
to the Ponte Angelo. They leave with Bruno. The Pope orders
a feast to be prepared to celebrate Saint Peter's day and his
own victory.

The effect of Faustus's invisibility is soon felt. The entrance
of the real cardinals is fraught with expectation after the
dialogue between Faustus and Mephostophilis. And the buffoonery is soon set in motion. Faustus triumphs, but the
comedy has something of a black flavour, since the Pope is
fooled and deliberately diminished by the actions. Ceremonial
is destroyed, apparently from within. The difference in style
and effect from any other part of the play has cast doubt upon
the authenticity of this writing. But Faustus has always shown
such a capacity to abuse his purchased power in particularly
frivolous ways – almost a mark of his character escaping from
the ominous results of his commitment, that it is possible
Marlowe intended to merge entertainment and criticism. The
groundlings would respond to this, while the more educated

would enjoy the destruction of Roman Catholic ceremonial and, by analogy, inherent mockery of the Catholic Church.

Maro Publius Vergilius Maro was the full name of the Roman poet Virgil. He acquired during the Middle Ages a reputation for magic powers, hence the next two lines.

sumptuous temple St Mark's, Venice. In spite of the richness of its architecture and decoration, it harmonizes in size with the Piazza San Marco in which it is situated, rather than impressing one by its height.

stream River.

Ponte Bridge. Next to it is the castle of St Angelo.

pyramides Marlowe means obelisk.

Of Styx, of Acheron ... Phlegethon The rivers of Hades, the underworld of the dead in Greek myth.

triumphs Festival shows.

antics Buffoons. The word is also used in this sense in Shakespeare.

crosiers Staffs surmounted by a cross, carried before the bishops on ceremonial occasions.

pillars Carried before the cardinals, as were the crosiers before the bishops.

procession The Processional is a service book containing prayers and hymns suitable for use during a religious procession.

state pontifical Papal throne.

flourish A prelude performed on trumpets; here it indicates the approach of the Pope. 'A flourish' had the same meaning as 'a sennet' (see our Note, p. 58).

feet ... hands A reference to a contemporary proverb.

consistory Where the cardinals gather in formal meeting.

decretal The laws decreed or laid down by the councils, such as the Council of Trent, which sat from 1545 to 1563 (after the time of Faustus).

synod A meeting of bishops and cardinals.

let me ... law Grant that I have some legal right.

interdict Ban.

Pope Alexander ... German Frederick Pope Alexander III forced the Emperor Frederick to submit to him when the Emperor's son had been captured. The Emperor had established a rival Pope: Victor IV. This is a parallel situation to that described here with Bruno.

progenitor Predecessor.

basilisk. A serpent in fable, whose eyes possessed the power to kill.

schismatic One responsible for a split in the Church.

Sigismund Marlowe has confused the historical facts. Pope Julius and the Emperor Sigismund belonged to quite different times.

keys The keys given to St Peter.

quittance Recompense.

lollards Those who followed the heretical opinions of John
  Wyclif (1324–84), a forerunner of the Reformation and a
  translator of the Bible.

Ponte Angelo A castle on the Tiber.

college An assembly of cardinals.

again To come back.

Scene 9

Faustus and Mephostophilis attend the Pope's banquet.
Bruno is now on his way to the Emperor in Germany. The
Pope, the Lords and the Cardinals enter. There is some confusion between Pope and Cardinals as a result of Faustus
and Mephostophilis having previously taken the places of the
latter. The Pope threatens the Cardinals with death unless
they imprison Bruno and the Emperor. The Pope asks his
guests to sit down to the feast. Faustus plays his pranks: he
snatches a present given by the Bishop of Milan; a dish sent
by a French Cardinal; and the Pope's wine. He then boxes the
Pope's ear. The Pope leaves, and the Friars enter with bell,
book and candle to curse whoever was responsible for the
deeds against the Pope.

Mephostophilis is triumphant at the success of the ploy
with Bruno, and Faustus's assumption of invisibility via his
magic prepares us for the sick humour bordering on farce
which constitutes the main ingredient of the scene. The invocation is in rhymed couplets to produce an incantatory
effect. There is dramatic tension as the cardinals are fooled,
and farce in Faustus's snatches. 'The ghost out of purgatory'
is a significant reference to the omnipresence of evil, while the
farce continues with the letting off of the fireworks. Note the
speed of the action in this scene – the audience is kept
constantly involved because of it.

forked hair Probably a reference to the snakes' tongues of which
  the Furies' hair consists.

Pluto's blue fire The flames of the underworld, of which Pluto is
  the god.

Hecate Cf. *Macbeth*, Act 4, Scene 1, where Hecate appears to the
  three witches.

fall to Eat heartily.

adry Dry.

lubbers Awkward fools.

aware Beware.

soul The ghost that is assumed to be causing the trouble.

took ... a blow Gave a blow.

pardon An indulgence to pardon sins. It was the impudent sale of indulgences that was one of the causes of the Reformation. Chaucer's Pardoner is an example.

aware Be warned of.

with bell, book, and candle The exercise of exorcism, the form of which includes the use of the bell, the book of offices, and the putting out of three candles.

Dirge The word is inaccurately used to refer to a service of excommunication. (It really means 'a Mass for the dead'.)

maledicat Dominus ... Et omnes Sancti! (Latin). May the Lord curse him! And all the Saints!

Scene 10

This scene is a variation of Scene ix in the A text where Robin and Dick (Ralph in the A text) cheat the Vintner of his cup and summon up an indignant Mephostophilis, who changes Dick (Ralph) into an ape and Robin into a dog.

The theft of the cup is again parody (here of Faustus stealing the wine from the Pope), and provides the opportunity for much word-play between the rustics and Vintner. Their conjurations are also parody, and the irritation of Mephostophilis leads to prompt and unpleasant action, though surprisingly the pair show no fear of the devil.

at the hard heels Close behind.

outface ... matter Impudently argue with me.

beyond us Neither now possesses the cup.

shrewd Bad.

tester A coin of small value.

Chorus 2

The Chorus describes how Faustus returns home after seeing many fine sights and royal courts. His friends welcome his return, question him about astrology, and are lost in wonder at his knowledge and skills. His fame spreads through all lands. The Emperor Charles V invites Faustus to his palace, to display his powers.

Again functional, noting Faustus's fame but preparing for the scenes at the Emperor's court where he will show just how skilled are his occult powers.

gratulate Congratulate.
Carolus the Fifth Charles V, Holy Roman Emperor from 1519
to 1556. Upon his abdication his kingdom was divided and he
retired to a monastery.

Scene 11

Martino and Frederick enter and speak of Faustus's fame in
the magic art. He intends to conjure up for the Emperor
Charles the shapes of Alexander and his mistress. Benvolio
appears at a window above in his nightcap. He has a low
opinion of the wonders that Faustus has promised to perform.

This marks the passage of time and is an underlining of
Faustus's reputation: it prepares us for what is to come. An
interesting emphasis is that Faustus, agent of the devil, is
feared by Martino and Frederick but is cynically regarded by
Benvolio.

voided Evacuated.
consort Go with.
took his rouse Drank a lot.
post Go quickly.
compass'd Achieved.
control Overcome.

Scene 12

This scene is a variation of a similar scene in the A text, where
Faustus summons the shapes of Alexander and his mistress to
appear before the Emperor. There are additional characters in
the Court, such as Bruno. Benvolio takes the part of the
unnamed knight, assuming a much fuller part in subsequent
scenes. The dumb-show includes Alexander's fight with
Darius.

The Emperor speaks highly of Faustus's skill in magic, but
asks for some proof of the reports he has heard. Faustus replies
with a due affectation of modesty. As he does so, Benvolio
mocks him from the side. The Emperor asks to see Alexander
and his mistress. Benvolio keeps up his comments, Faustus
notes them and tells the Emperor that the 'royal shapes'
must be treated with silence. The dumb show follows and then
the horns are fixed on Benvolio's head.

Benvolio remaining in the window and commenting on
Faustus's reception is a clever dramatic device, since he is in

fact voicing what the audience knows but what the characters do not know. The conjurations also have a double function – they would be appreciated by the German Court and the contemporary audience alike for their spectacle. The effect is of a play within the play, with the dumb show separated from human reaction. The treatment of Benvolio is direct evidence of the power of evil, though Faustus's letting him off is ironically charged with an approximation of Christian mercy. Comparison is invited with the ass's head worn by Bottom in *A Midsummer's Night's Dream*.

hale Drag.
Compass Achieve.
paramour Lover.
an If.
Zounds By God's wounds.
Actaeon ... Diana Actaeon found Diana bathing while he was hunting. She changed him into a stag and he was torn to pieces by his dogs.
footmanship Ability to run quickly.
Belimote, Argiron, Asterote These references are corruptions of other names: probably 'Behemoth', a monster; Acheron, the infernal regions or a river in Hades; Ashtaroth a goddess.
anon Soon.
injurious Insulting.
smooth faces Boys (scholars).

Revision questions, Scenes 6–12

1 Faustus makes poor use of the powers for which he has bartered his soul. Discuss.
2 In the opening scenes Faustus was a scholar and a gentleman; in the middle scenes he is little better than a buffoon. How far is this statement true?
3 Faustus who had aspired to be level with God has become a magician who uses his powers to entertain himself and others. Discuss.
4 Comment on the quality of humour in scenes with the Pope and Emperor.
5 This part of the play has little function in terms of plot except to indicate the passage of time. Discuss.

Scene 13

Benvolio is intent on revenge. He discusses this with Martino and Frederick, who attempt to dissuade him. With the soldiers, however, they determine to kill Faustus. He enters with a false head, which they strike off. He cannot be killed during his twenty-four years on earth, as he tells them when, to their consternation, he gets up. He commands Mephostophilis and other Devils to punish those who have attempted to kill him. When Faustus is attacked by the soldiers, he places a barrier between himself and them.

A dramatic scene imbued with passion on the part of Benvolio – the revenge motif which is a major part of Elizabethan tragedy from Kyd's *The Spanish Tragedy* through to Shakespeare's *Hamlet* is here reduced to a farcical emphasis. In a sense, the introduction of rhyming couplets undercuts any realism which the audience might expect. The dramatic effects are achieved by the farce (the head falling off) and then Faustus's revenge, the positive antidote to Benvolio's. The end of the scene is symbolic in a farcical sense, of evil triumphing over good with the humiliation of the soldiers.

let slip Ignore.
But Except.
quit Wipe out, repay.
close Concealed.
policy Plan, trick.
dally Play with.
He ... drives A contemporary proverbial saying.
remove Move.
incontinent Straightaway.

Scene 14

Benvolio, Frederick and Martino enter with their heads and faces bleeding, covered with dirt, and all wearing horns. They decide to retire to Benvolio's castle to hide their shame.

The rhyming couplets used by Benvolio and Frederick with their easy rhythms add to the farcical nature of the scene. But when they appear 'besmeared with mud and dirt; all having horns on their heads', Marlowe combines natural blank verse with interspersed rhyming lines which somehow heighten the effect of suffering.

to kill A play on the horns and the killing of animals with horns in the hunt.
sped Finished.
spite of spite In spite of everything.
Sith Since.

Scene 15

A brief scene in which Faustus swindles the horse-dealer, and further tricks him by his conjuring skill.

The scene with the horse-courser is common or garden swindling: having exposed the Court and the nobility, Faustus extends his trickery to the other end of the social scale. Though there is an element of black humour about this – the purchaser of nothing is a poor man – Faustus reveals his conscience, his sense of his own numbered days, in a short soliloquy which is made poignant by his attempts to escape into sleep. There is a swift degeneration into slapstick with the pulling off of the leg, made all the more effective by the transition from Faustus's 'Tush, Christ did call the thief upon the cross', a direct reference to Luke 23: 43 where Christ promises 'This day shalt thou be with me in Paradise'.

Horse-courser Horse-dealer.
fatal time The time ruled by fate.
call Promise salvation.
in conceit I.e., be content.
cozening Swindling.
scab Villain.
no niggard Not mean or sparing.

Scene 16

Robin discusses his credit with the hostess. The carter describes how he sold a load of as much hay as Faustus could eat; he ate the whole load which had been purchased for a ludicrously small sum. The horse-courser describes how Faustus had sold him a horse which, when he rode it into the water, turned into a bottle of hay, and how later they had pulled off Faustus's leg.

The emphasis here is on the grotesque (and trivial in one sense) nature of Faustus's exploits. Notice here a favourite Marlowe device – the reportage of incident (even to repetition) which fixes in the mind of the audience Faustus's temporary power. We are also inclined to ask *why* Faustus employs himself in this silly way – it is almost as if he is not making the most of his measured time.

on the score In debt.
still There is a play on meaning here between 'still' in the sense of not growing and not decreasing by being paid.

cursen Christian.
brave Splendid.

Scene 17

The beginning of this scene with the Duke of Vanholt and the grapes is similar in both texts. The B text adds the comic matter at the end, where Robin, Dick, the carter and horse-courser meet Faustus and provide, with the hostess, more amusement for the Duke of Vanholt and his Duchess. At the Duke's palace a dish of ripe grapes appears for the Duchess. Faustus explains that grapes are in season in the east, and that is where these grapes have been procured.

This scene, a conflation of two scenes perhaps, is curiously mixed. But at the same time the style has its own closeness of texture, linking grapes, raisins and figs, with a pun on 'reason' and 'raisin'. This is the end of the comic sequence, with Faustus going through his repertoire of tricks, persuasive, conning, then taking on the rustics in an extended prose exchange, and working his magic on them.

great-bellied Many pregnant women have longings for particular foods.
circle The northern and southern hemispheres: Marlowe's geographical knowledge is weak at this point.
Saba Sheba.
bounce Hammer.
coil Din.
Commit Send to prison. Dick gives the meaning a sexual significance.
sauce-box Impudence.
gage Stake.
stand much upon A play on the literal meaning and not placing much weight upon.
colussus The Colussus of Rhodes was thought to stand astride the entrance to the harbour.
carry it away Carry it off.
hey-pass ... re-pass Expressions used by jugglers and conjurers during their acts.

Scene 18

Wagner thinks that Faustus will soon die as he has be-queathed all his goods to him. Yet Faustus still leads a riotous life, feasting and drinking with the students. Faustus enters with several scholars; they have been discussing who was the most beautiful woman in the world and have decided that it was Helen of Greece. They beseech Faustus to make Helen appear for them; Faustus obliges and Helen appears briefly. They leave, astonished by her beauty. An Old Man appears, to implore Faustus to seek Christ's mercy. Faustus despairs; he is certain of his damnation. He contemplates suicide and Mephostophilis hands him a dagger. The Old Man urges him to avoid despair and seek mercy. As the Old Man leaves he holds out little hope for Faustus's salvation. When Mephostophilis threatens to punish Faustus for thinking of mercy and repentance Faustus is immediately contrite. He asks Mephostophilis to help him overcome his thoughts about salvation by bringing him Helen to satisfy his desires. Helen appears and Faustus is enraptured by her beauty. She represents the consummation of all his desires, all his aspirations and all his ideas of beauty. Other matters are forgotten, and the Old Man laments Faustus's fate.

In returning the scene to Faustus's study Marlowe prepares us for the inevitable conclusion. The structure of the play has come full circle. Wagner's words prefigure the end, but the main dramatic stroke is the conjuration of Helen of Troy. The entrance of the Old Man (Faustus will never be an old man) is a cunning use of contrast: his speech is full of quiet dignity. Notice the effective use of the word 'bereave', which underlines the spiritual death which awaits Faustus. There is some fine close work here, with the juxtaposition of 'The sight of heaven' and 'The pains of hell'. Faustus would repent if he could, but 'Hell strives with grace' and with the appearance of Helen he is lost. Note the sensuality of 'Her lips suck forth my soul' with its erotic language and sense of passionate physical contact. Ironically Faustus sees himself as a knight fighting for his lady: the imagery of the blank verse, steeped in classical allusion, describes Helen in terms of bright, celestial beauty. Adjectives and alliterative effects cohere, as in 'plumed' and 'flaming', and 'Arethusa's azured arms'. The Old Man's re-entrance emphasizes that it is too late, for Faustus's sensuality has ensured his eternal damnation. Here the role of Mephostophilis is crucial; his re-conjuring of Helen effectively seals Faustus's fate. The Old Man, who represents Christian repentance, is inviolable, the devils cannot harm him: ominously, they have come to take possession of Faustus.

Sir Paris A medieval mode of address, applied to a classical hero.

Dardania Troy.

rape Carrying off.

Revolt Return (to Lucifer).

drift Delay.

topless So high that the tops could not be seen.

Menelaus He was the husband of Helen whom Paris carried off, thus causing the Trojan War. After the war Menelaus and Helen were reunited and lived at Sparta. There is no clear reason for the use of 'weak'. When he fought Paris he would have slain him had Paris not been carried off by Aphrodite.

achilles According to Homer, Achilles was wounded in the right arm. Achilles was reputed to be invulnerable except in the heel by which his mother held him when she dipped him in the river Styx.

hapless Semele She asked Zeus to visit her as a god. He came in his splendour and Semele perished in the flames.

monarch of the sky The Sun.

In wanton Arethusa's azur'd arms Caressed unrestrainedly in the blue waters. Arethusa was the nymph of the fountain of Arethusa on the island of Ortygia.

sift Make trial of.

pride Glorious power.

Scene 19

Lucifer, Beelzebub and Mephostophilis discuss Faustus's impending fate, and linger to observe him during the remainder of the scene. Faustus and Wagner then enter, speaking about Faustus's will.

The end approaches; Faustus speaks to the scholars about his fate. He realizes that his sin has led to his damnation. The scholars urge him to look to heaven and call on God. Faustus once more despairs; his sin is the one that can never be pardoned. He has been led astray by knowledge; the wonders he has performed will not save him from hell. He has surrendered his soul for knowledge and for the pleasure of twenty-four years – now his time is up. If he names God, the devil will tear him to pieces: he begs them to leave him if they do not wish to share his fate. His friends are loyal to him, and promise to pray that God will have mercy on him. As the clock strikes eleven Faustus has but one hour to live before he is for ever damned. He implores time to stand still, so that he may still save his soul, but time moves on. One drop of Christ's blood would save him. He wishes that the mountains and the hills would fall on him to hide him from God's anger. Neither the earth nor the clouds hold any refuge for Faustus. The clock strikes the half-hour; Faustus still implores God's mercy and asks, in the name of Christ, for some limit to his damnation. He envies the beasts for whom death is the end and for whom there is no eternal damnation. He curses himself, and Lucifer who has deprived him of the joys of heaven. The clock strikes twelve, hell gapes for Faustus and the Devils bear him away.

Marlowe builds towards the play's climax a scene full of urgency and desperation. The thunder and the reigning devils strike the ominous note, and this is followed by the short sharp dialogue between Faustus and the scholars, which is full of tension. It is ironic that Faustus's quest for knowledge has lost him his soul, whereas the scholars, also pursuing knowledge, are still full of faith. The intense seriousness here contrasts with the triviality, jokey scenes and tricks which characterize so much of Faustus's earlier behaviour. We are aware of the inexorable movement of time as the clock strikes, and this sense of movement is heightened by the succession of verbs – move, runs, will strike. The dramatic language is heightened by exclamations, while Faustus's final speech is charged with fine poetry. The various magical effects and tricks, and the presentation, so vivid, of Hell, make this scene immediately present – the speech is breathless with fear, despair, final rejection.

chamber-fellow A student sharing the same chamber.
serpent See Genesis, 3, 1–15.
nature's eye The Sun.
O lente . . . equi O run slowly, slowly, you horses of the night. From Ovid's *Amores* which Marlowe had translated. Ovid wishes to extend the hours of love; this makes its use in this context ironic.
Where is it now The idea of salvation through Christ's blood had gone as a result of his invocation to Lucifer.
influence In astrology, the position of the stars at birth is held to influence the pattern of life.
Pythagoras' *metempsychosis* Pythagoras was a Greek philosopher and mathematician (540–510 BC). He taught the transmigration of souls from man to beast. Cf. Shakespeare's *Twelfth Night*, 4, 2, 49–51:
Feste 'What is the opinion of Pythagoras concerning wild fowl?'
Malvolio 'That the soul of our grandam might haply inhabit a bird.'

Scene 20

This is an additional scene in the B text. The scholars comment on the dreadful night that has just passed. They find Faustus dead and torn apart. The third scholar recalls Faustus's cry for help after midnight, when the house seemed as if it were on fire. They resolve to give Faustus a fitting burial.

The emphasis is on Christian compassion and forgiveness, thus contrasting with the action of the play and Faustus's damnation.

Epilogue: *Enter* Chorus

The Chorus enters to lament Faustus's fate and the sense of loss and waste it represents. His fate is a warning against the desire to meddle with unlawful things that heaven has forbidden.

God's will be done – the plain statement echoes the morality plays which Marlowe obviously used to emphasize his own structure.

Apollo's laurel bough Apollo was the Greek god of poetry; the laurel was a mark of distinction given to poets.
Only to wonder at i.e. not to act or dabble in 'unlawful things'.
Terminat hora ... opus (Latin). The hour ends the day, the author ends his work.

Revision questions, Scenes 12–end

1 Whatever may be the defects of the middle part of the play, the end is tragedy of the highest order. Discuss this judgement of the final part.
2 What part is played by the apparition of Helen?
3 Why does Faustus not repent?
4 Describe the significance of the appearances of the Old Man.
5 What do we learn about the character of Faustus from the way in which he faces up to his imminent death, in the scene with the scholars, and in his last hour?

The characters

Doctor Faustus

Yet art thou still but Faustus and a man.

Faustus is, overwhelmingly, the central character of the play: the attention of the audience is focused upon him to a degree that is found in few other plays. In *Hamlet*, for example, the audience is predominantly interested in the thoughts and actions of the hero, but there exists also a range of other characters who are convincing in themselves and who have a lively and revealing relationship with Hamlet. In *Doctor Faustus* this is not so. Faustus is not only the hero around whom the play revolves: he is also, apart from Mephostophilis, the only real *individual* and has no significant relationship with any other character – again apart from Mephostophilis.

This lack of interaction between Faustus and other characters leads inevitably to a lack of fullness in the depiction of Faustus's own character – one of the most important ways of revealing a character is by observing him in relationship with others.

There is the feeling in *Doctor Faustus* that the hero is being presented and analysed as both a concept and a man. That is why there has been, to this day, so much critical writing about the specific nature of Faustus's sin; about whether repentance is possible for him; and about the nature and value of his compact with Lucifer. These are all external to the essential personality of the human being.

Plainly Marlowe identified closely with his hero. But to assert that Faustus is Marlowe is to ignore the workings of the creative mind and to forget that Marlowe was a dramatist very concerned with writing plays for a specific theatre and audience. Faustus's outlook and aspirations may have a good deal in common with those of Marlowe. He was a young man when he wrote *Doctor Faustus*, even though the play was written at the end of his life; and as a dramatist he lacked the objectivity that can be found in the mature Shakespeare or Jonson. The cast of his mind was clearly intellectual. The lyrical vied with the dramatic in his poetic expression. These qualities, even within the framework of the drama, inevitably lead to a large measure of subjectivity. However, the biography of Marlowe will not do much to illuminate the character of Faustus. So little is known of Marlowe's life that it is rather through his portrayal of Faustus that we will learn something of Marlowe.

Faustus is a scholar. It is significant that when he removes the horns from the Knight's head, he does not mention the Knight's insults about his magical powers; he simply warns him hereafter to 'speak well of scholars'. Much of the play is spent in Faustus's study: like so many outstanding men who were humbly born, it was through learning that he was able to rise above his lowly beginnings.

Faustus was born of poor parents in Rhode in Germany. He was chiefly brought up by relatives who sent him to university at Wittenberg. Here he excelled in the study of divinity, and was awarded his doctorate. He was so outstanding in scholarship and in learned argument that he grew proud of himself and his powers. At the beginning of the play he is no longer content with the pursuit of knowledge: he has studied all the main branches of the learning of his time, and is satisfied by none of them. He demands more from logic than the ability it gives one in debate. Medicine has brought him fame and riches but confers upon him only human powers. The study of law is for slaves and leads to nothing significant. Divinity is preferable to these, but cannot get beyond sin and death. It is *magic* that promises to open up new worlds of power and to make man into a god.

Here we see the three character defects in Faustus that led to his ultimate domination by Mephostophilis: his overweening pride; his restless intellect; and his desire to be more than man, to possess the power and the insight of a god.

Aristotle laid down that the tragic hero is a predominantly good man, whose undoing is brought about by some error of human frailty: 'the stamp of one defect'. Any one of these three defects of Faustus would have been sufficient to ensure his downfall in terms of the theory of tragedy. In his pride he is guilty of *hubris*, a quality which in Greek tragedy was certain to arouse the wrath of the gods. His desire to be equated with God is a sin in Christian terms. His restless intellect and deep dissatisfaction with the normality of life inevitably lead to misfortune.

Step by step Faustus falls into damnation. The compact with Lucifer is the logical and inevitable conclusion to what has gone before. In some ways Faustus's aspirations are admirable. It was the glory and the ambition of the Renaissance man to have an 'aspiring mind'. Faustus, on one level, represents the new man emerging from the womb of the Middle Ages. The authority of the Church, which had limited the thought of the Middle Ages, was lessening. There was a movement of power from Church to State, which meant, to a limited extent, the transfer of power to the individual man. The classical spirit was a source of influence, certainly to Marlowe and some of his fellow dramatists, the 'university wits'. The Greek attitude to their gods was very different from that of the medieval Church. The Greeks encouraged a spirit of enquiry in their thought that was quite foreign to the attitude of the medieval Church. Greek thought was not, of course, completely unfettered; the death of Socrates showed that philosophy was not without its risks.

This is the key to much of the duality of Faustus's thought and attitudes. He looks sometimes backwards to the medieval period and sometimes forwards to the modern world. Above all, he is an Elizabethan, adventurously exploring a world whose horizons were widening every day as a result of the explorations of their travellers and voyagers. Richard Hakluyt's *Principal Navigations, Voyages, Traffiques, and Discoveries of the English Nation, made by Sea or over Land* was one of the most popular books of the day. Faustus himself is full of this excitement in geographical discovery. Protestantism, while it had its own orthodoxy (which could at times be ruthlessly and cruelly insisted upon), represented a revolt against the Roman Church, which had dominated thought. The escapade with the Pope demonstrates that Faustus is a good Elizabethan Protestant in feeling.

The Elizabethans – in contrast with men of the immediately succeeding and preceding ages – were in love with life and its possibilities. They lived dangerously but whole-heartedly; they enjoyed their literature, their music and even their art, though this was on a lower level and had become secular. Fundamentally, Faustus's choice is Elizabethan, not medieval – he sacrifices eternity for twenty-four years of full life now – yet the authority of the Middle Ages and the Church remains. *Doctor Faustus* opens in a spirit of rebellion; it closes in one of orthodoxy. This is the basic conflict in the mind of Faustus, a man caught between two worlds.

Faustus's closest relationship is with the scholars. They have an admiration for him and a genuine concern for his welfare, and they are afraid for him when they hear of his association with Valdes and Cornelius. He is on sufficiently intimate terms with the scholars to discuss the fears induced by his approaching death, and they do their best to comfort him. Faustus is prepared to oblige them by causing Helen to appear before them.

Faustus is an intellectual, concerned with discovering the truth; his lively curiosity covers many fields of learning and knowledge. His questing mind is concerned with principles, purposes and the essence of things, rather than with appearances and mere workings. He is often dissatisfied with the answers of Mephostophilis, whom he sometimes angers by querying fundamental principles. Faustus is concerned with the reality behind the appearance, yet he is frequently naive in his approach. Concerned deeply with the truth of things outside himself, he lacks self-knowledge. He demands that Mephostophilis shall reveal to him the secrets of astronomy, but when Mephostophilis talks to him about the realities of hell, Faustus can only mock him for his lack of manly fortitude. He has an almost childish delight in his powers as a conjuror of devils, but, as Mephostophilis points out, the 'conjuring speeches' were the accidental, not the real reason for his appearing to Faustus. They are, he adds, powers which even Faustus' servant Wagner can use to his own advantage.

One of the strange contradictions in the character of Faustus lies in his combination of scholar and buffoon. The one has dignity and tragic nobility, the other is crude, immature and petty. These contradictions existed in the audience too, and were to some extent, we may infer, a part of the Elizabethan character − shared by individuals as well as existing in the general consciousness. It was a violent age, given to extremes of contrast: callous towards suffering yet at times gentle and considerate; there was the exquisite sensibility of its musical taste, the beauty of the madrigal, and the barbarity of the public executions. One should not, therefore, be too surprised by Faustus's perception and appreciation of Helen's beauty and his delight in boxing the ears of the Pope, or executing a jest on the Horse-courser. Some of these scenes may not, of course, have been written by Marlowe; nevertheless, they must be considered in our estimate of the character of Faustus.

The weakness in the delineation of Faustus's character in these particular scenes is that the situation dominates the characterization. When Hamlet is involved in a comic scene it is dominated by *him*. The gravediggers are a couple of clowns, but their dialogue with Hamlet mirrors the prevailing atmosphere of the play, and the consistent unity of Hamlet's character is maintained. This is not so with Faustus; his character is submerged in the farce.

It is a commonplace of criticism to state that Faustus has little enjoyment or satisfaction from his acquired powers. This is a problem of character; it is also a question of human limitation. Faustus's desire for knowledge cannot be satisfied because Marlowe himself cannot represent what he does not know; nor is it necessary in the theatre that he should.

In one sense, Faustus is satisfied. Mephostophilis refuses to give him a wife, but he does promise him possession of any woman he desires. His longings find their consummation in Helen. This represents an important facet of Faustus's character: his willingness to carry things to an ultimate conclusion. In his conjuring it was he who took the final step in which Cornelius and Valdes were happy to instruct but not to share. So it is with Helen. She may be a consolation but she is also his damnation. She is a spirit, as Faustus has pointed out when he summons the likenesses of Alexander and his paramour for the Emperor. She is a spirit raised by the devil, and therefore, one may presume, a spirit of evil. To have intercourse with such a spirit was an extreme sin; much later than this, witches were burnt on similar grounds. After this incident there is no further appearance of the Good and Evil Angels, who keep alive throughout the play the possibility of salvation; and the words of the Old Man, after Faustus praises Helen, show the hopelessness of Faustus's fate.

There is, however, a commendable aspect to his character shown in this relationship: there is no indication anywhere that Faustus uses people for his own pleasure. Unlike Goethe's Faust, he does not select and desert an innocent maid like Gretchen, nor does he revel in lust for its own sake. He chooses as the object of his desire the most beautiful woman the world has ever known. Sinful it may be, degrading it is not.

Faustus is given to bouts of despair. Mephostophilis, despite his own rather melancholy disposition, tries to cheer him by a series of 'spectaculars'. Even Lucifer provides the 'show' of the Seven Deadly Sins. This may spring from Marlowe's own 'Satanic readings of life', referred to by Una Ellis-Fermor as 'his own inarticulate and hardly acknowledged conviction that it is evil.' Faustus is often excited by life; he is determined to live it to the full, but he is unhappy in it. This melancholy and despair may well have influenced his agreement to the compact.

When we speak of damnation and repentance, we must be careful that we understand *Doctor Faustus* aright. In itself the temptation is towards avoiding, not accepting, damnation. In the conversation with Mephostophilis, there is a manic excitement that leaves Faustus's course in no doubt; even after that, much of the conflict is externalized in the Good and Evil Angels, unless we view these as facets of the mind of Faustus. There is in him no serious motivation towards good; when he speaks of it, the reference is always outside himself. He does not seek a genuine relationship with Christ or with God; it is Christ's blood he sees as something apart, streaming in the firmament. He is concerned, at the end, with the clock and with time, rather than with the reality of God. The Old Man triumphs over the Devils; Faustus succumbs easily to the threats of Mephostophilis. There is a prevailing feeling that evil has power over him because he is fascinated by its conflict with good, and by the powers it promises.

Some see in Faustus's end an element of cowardice, an inability to face the consequences of his compact and his life; others see in it the essential nobility of tragedy. The situation itself is the very stuff of tragedy. How Faustus came to be there does not detract from the tragic moment, which Marlowe exploits to the full. Faustus becomes a Prometheus-like figure, symbolizing man caught in the net of eternity. Just as Faustus throughout the play has been unable to accept the limitations imposed upon man by the nature of human life, the world and the social order in which it is lived, so, in his last moments, he struggles at the same time to resolve and escape from the idea of eternity – which means for him eternal damnation. He is honest here as elsewhere. He places the blame upon himself and upon Lucifer and, in the desire to burn his books, recognizes that his pride of knowledge and his insatiable curiosity have led to his damnation.

The Chorus leaves us with the tragic sense of waste. Faustus, who might have been a force for good, remains as a warning to those who desire a power beyond what God is prepared to grant.

Mephostophilis

I am a servant to great Lucifer.

Many literary critics avow that it is far easier to create evil characters than good ones. In Milton's *Paradise Lost* it is Satan, in all his pride and energy, who makes the greatest impact on the reader. Marlowe did not, however, share Milton's problem; Faustus and Mephostophilis do not represent good and evil. Faustus is, in one sense, like Mephostophilis, on the devil's side; Mephostophilis is not without his good qualities.

Mephostophilis is bluntly honest with Faustus from his very first appearance. Faustus is overwhelmed with joy at his appearance and is delighted at his obedience in returning, at Faustus's command, dressed as a Franciscan friar: 'How pliant is this Mephostophilis,/Full of obedience and humility!' he exclaims. He is full of pride at his powers in conjuring that can command 'great Mephostophilis' – who, however, quickly points out to him that Lucifer is his master and he cannot follow Faustus without Lucifer's permission. He also disillusions Faustus about the effectiveness of the 'conjuring speeches' Faustus has made. Mephostophilis has arrived in the hope of gaining Faustus's soul, rather than as a result of the conjuring.

Mephostophilis deals fairly and honestly with Faustus. He makes no attempt to gloss over the position of Lucifer, whose fall was brought about 'by aspiring pride and insolence,/For which God threw him from the face of heaven'. He refers to himself as one of the 'Unhappy spirits that fell with Lucifer'. He indicates that his damnation is eternal, and that heaven is immeasurably to be preferred to hell:

Why, this is hell, nor am I out of it:
Think'st thou that I, who saw the face of God
And tasted the eternal joys of heaven,
Am not tormented with ten thousand hells
In being depriv'd of everlasting bliss?

Mephostophilis's honest realism evokes a charge of cowardice from the excited Faustus, who urges him to learn 'manly fortitude'. For Faustus, Mephostophilis remains the glorious means whereby he is going to be 'great emp'ror of the world'. But the expectation, the ultimate disappointment and the final tragedy spring wholly from Faustus; they are not inspired by any dishonesty or false promises on the part of Mephostophilis.

Once the pact is made Mephostophilis carries out his side of the bargain faithfully, albeit somewhat disappointingly in terms of Faustus's expectations. In addition to satisfying Faustus's intellectual curiosity, he attempts to keep him entertained. He remains wholly honest on the subjects of hell and damnation, and it is on these subjects that he rises, like Milton's Satan, to his greatest nobility, expressed in powerful verse: 'Hell hath no limits, nor is circumscrib'd/In one self place, but where we are is hell,/And where hell is, there must we ever be'. Mephostophilis expresses the basic thought of Renaissance man, breaking the bounds of medieval ecclesiastical thought and asserting in the true spirit of humanism the essential glory of man: 'But think'st thou heaven is such a glorious thing?/I tell thee, Faustus, it is not half so fair/As thou or any man that breathes on earth'.

Mephostophilis is no moralist; he will have nothing to do with the conventional morality of marriage, which he regards as 'but a ceremonial toy'. He promises Faustus that he can have any woman he desires, no matter how chaste, wise or beautiful she may be, and indeed does a fine job in producing for him Helen, the most beautiful woman of all time.

He is less successful in satisfying Faustus's intellectual curiosity and Faustus complains about the answers to his questions on the universe: 'These slender questions Wagner can decide:/Hath Mephostophilis no greater skill?' In the serious parts of the play he maintains his dignity and a certain nobility; in the farcical episodes he becomes a quite different character. When he extols the delights of Rome he sounds like a tours guide, even to the point of being tedious. He may have Protestant sympathies, for he shares all the Elizabethan hatred for the friars, not only condemning their gluttony but obviously enjoying helping Faustus to beat them, and flinging fireworks among them.

Mephostophilis is something of an aristocrat. He has no objection to being the servant of Faustus, whose soul would be a fine prize, but he disapproves strongly of being brought from Constantinople at the bidding of Ralph and Robin, who are turned into an ape and a dog respectively for their pains. He is, however, still capable of enjoying the coarse farce in the scene with the Horse-courser, and delights in startling him when the Horse-courser pulls away Faustus's leg. It is difficult to maintain an unchanging concept of the character throughout all the comic scenes; plainly some of these were not written by Marlowe, and Mephostophilis becomes a stock figure of comedy, reminiscent of similar figures in the morality and miracle plays. He merely fulfils a role in the comedy; his character is not the concern of the writer or writers of these scenes.

Towards the end of the play the relationship between Mephostophilis and Faustus changes, as does the character of Mephostophilis. Instead of providing the despairing Faustus with some amusement to distract him, he gives him a dagger. He is dictatorial towards Faustus when there is a danger of repentance, and threatens to tear him apart if he does not remain faithful to Lucifer.

The name of Mephostophilis is the last word Faustus utters before he dies. This is as it should be, for it is he who has been the companion of Faustus in his passage towards damnation. It is Mephostophilis who, in stage terms, gives reality to and externalizes the damnation of Faustus. He symbolizes the damnation and intensifies the conflict in Faustus between the losing and the saving of his soul. He is at once servant, companion, master, teacher and entertainer. He is not, except in an external sense, the destroyer of Faustus; Faustus does that for himself.

Wagner

Wagner is Faustus's servant. He plays little part in the serious scenes, but in the comic moments provides something of a foil to Faustus; he illustrates the crude and undignified use to which magic can be put and, in one sense, debases Faustus's achievement. If Wagner can conjure devils, then it is no great feat for Faustus to do so. Wagner can summon devils to his aid in order to succeed in petty matters (such as ensuring that the Clown enters his service). He is, like many servants, conscious of his own dignity – he insists on being called 'Master Wagner' and instructs the Clown to make sure that his right eye is always directly fixed on his master's left heel.

He has a certain impudence and wit which is demonstrated in his reception of the scholars; he is clever enough to imitate, and foolish enough to denigrate, the philosophers' academic jargon. In his final speech he shows a measure of sensitivity hitherto unrevealed, yet he remains puzzled by the discrepancy between Faustus's approaching end and his way of life. The relationship between Wagner and Faustus is casual and intermittent; he may ape his master, but he does not begin to understand him.

Minor characters

The Clown

Strictly a non-character, in the tradition of the stage clown. There may well have been an actor in the company for whom such a part had to be provided; though he had a very small role in the A text, in the 1616 (B) text he has a much larger part.

The Pope

It is doubtful whether Marlowe had any specific pope in mind. 'The Pope' is a symbol of those qualities in the Roman Catholic Church that led to the Reformation. There were several popes elected during the supposed lifetime of the historical, half-mythical Doctor Faustus, but Marlowe's venom is almost certainly directed at the contemporary papacy: Sixtus V was the pope at the time when *Doctor Faustus* was written.

The Cardinal of Lorraine

An actual historical personage: he plays a very insignificant part in the play.

The Emperor

See our Notes on the text.

The Duke of Vanholt

He and his Duchess are shadowy characters, puppets whose presence serves as an opportunity for Faustus to show his magical powers. According to *The Historie*, 'Vanholt' should be 'Anholt'. Marlowe follows very closely the account given in his source of Faustus's stay with the Duke and Duchess.

Valdes and Cornelius

They are instrumental in instructing Faustus in the rudiments of magic and the conjuring up of spirits. They both speak glowingly of the power and glory of magic and astrology, and begin by associating themselves with Faustus in the enterprise; they speak of 'we three', but, significantly, they do not join him when he conjures up Mephostophilis. Apparently they are not prepared to push their art to any real conclusion. There is no record of who Valdes was. For the background of Cornelius, see the Note on Agrippa in Scene 1.

Lucifer

The prince of Hell. The use of this name for Satan, the archangel who was hurled from heaven for rebelling against God, arises from a misunderstanding of a passage in *Isaiah*. Milton refers to him: 'his form had yet not lost/All her original brightness, nor appeared/Less than Archangel ruined' (*Paradise Lost* I, 591–4).

Marlowe's Lucifer is less majestic and terrible than Milton's. Mephostophilis, not Lucifer, is the key representative of evil in *Doctor Faustus*, yet when he speaks of Lucifer it is with something of Milton's majesty that his master is invested. His actual appearance in the play is disappointing, and his 'show' of the Seven Deadly Sins underlines the anticlimax in the appearance of the prince of Hell.

Helen

She makes two brief appearances and speaks not at all. For her background, see the Note on Menelaus, and for her part in the plot see the comments on the character of Faustus.

The Good and Evil Angels

The Angels are sometimes regarded as an externalization of the thoughts of Faustus; this is a 20th-century view, rather than a medieval one. The Angels are independent absolutes, one wholly good and one wholly evil; they appear in *Doctor Faustus* like allegorical figures of a morality play.

They reflect the possibility of both damnation and redemption being open to Faustus. A close examination shows that the Evil Angel declines in importance as the play advances and there is less need to urge the attractions of evil. They work by intellectual statement, by suggestion, and the Evil Angel by thrusts as well; the device of using the Angels at all is clumsy, but while acknowledging this, one must admit that Marlowe uses them to good effect.

The Old Man

He appears only at the end of the play when Faustus, in despair, is about to commit suicide. In the source book he is a neighbour; here he is a vague, allegorical figure utterly lacking in any individual traits of character. He is the pattern of the ideal Christian and takes the place of the Good Angel when he appears no more. He is a continuing reminder, even at this stage, of the possibility of repentance. He speaks coaxingly of 'the way of life,' and bluntly of the way of damnation: 'Of thy most vile and loathsome filthiness.' The blood of Christ, he asserts, can still save Faustus.

The Old man goes out sadly, for he can see no signs of repentance in Faustus. He it is, on his next and final appearance, who pronounces Faustus's inevitable doom. After Helen has appeared to Faustus the Old Man despairs. He witnesses and hears the major part of Faustus's lines in praise of Helen; his presence adds a further dimension to this speech. He symbolizes salvation through repentance and the mercy of Christ, at the very time that Faustus is uniting himself to Helen, the symbol of physical beauty, desire and the glory of the flesh. And he emphasizes the rejection by Faustus of heaven in favour of earthly delight, not with a living woman but with a manifestation produced by the powers of evil. Finally, the Old Man shows, by example, how evil and the devils can be resisted. In him good is the ultimate power: an ironic comment on Faustus's search for power through evil.

The Chorus

This is a well-known device of Greek drama. The function of the Chorus was to provide a link between the actors and the audience and to comment on the events of the play. In Elizabethan drama the device was occasionally used to set the scene and create atmosphere: Shakespeare's *Henry V* is one example.

In the opening speech here, the chorus prepares the audience for the subject of the play, gives the necessary early biography of Faustus, and sets the scene. He is the objective moral voice of the play. Even at this early stage he clearly outlines Faustus's fate and condemns him. The fate of Icarus is to be that of Faustus; he is 'such with cunning of a self-conceit'; he is to bring the wrath of heaven upon himself, he prefers magic before 'his chiefest bliss'.

The appearance of the Chorus after the Seven Deadly Sins is almost purely a dramatic convenience. There is an absence of moral judgement – indeed, there is a certain sense of excitement in the description of Faustus's journey round the universe and the journey to Rome 'upon a dragon's back'.

The Chorus returns again to testify to the affection of Faustus's friend and to the fame that he has gained by his knowledge and his power. Again the speech is morally neutral.

At the end he returns to his moral role, lamenting the sense of waste inherent in Faustus's fate and holding him up as a warning to others who might be so tempted.

There is no consistency of tone or purpose in the Chorus; Marlowe uses him as a dramatic convenience. There is no clear conception of his place in the play, and this may be the reason for the feeling of triteness and some insincerity left by this final speech. Following Faustus's final speech, it is a considerable anticlimax.

Structure and style

Marlowe was writing at a time of rapid development in style as well as in thought. He played an important part in this development of style; Swinburne, in a burst of enthusiasm, called him 'the father of English tragedy and the creator of English blank verse'. He was neither, as T. S. Eliot has pointed out. What he did – and it is no mean achievement – was to make *blank verse* a fitting instrument for the drama. It might have happened without Marlowe. Thomas Kyd in *The Spanish Tragedy* had shown that blank verse could be used effectively in drama, occasionally tedious and ranting though his style could be. What Marlowe specifically did was to extend the range of the dramatic uses of blank verse. In *Tamburlaine* the blank verse had been used largely on a rhetorical, bombastic level; but there was evidence also of a lyrical quality. The bombast of this blank verse found ready imitators – and critics.

However, in *Doctor Faustus* there is a substantial stylistic advance. The approach is less youthful and immature; there is the sense that he is considering the relationship between the verse and the dramatic effect he wishes to create. In *Tamburlaine* he had made the blank verse fit into his own individual mould but it lacked variety; in *Doctor Faustus* there is a good deal more variety in its dramatic use. *Tamburlaine* is significant for its use of the single line; in *Doctor Faustus* there is an attempt to subordinate the verse to the speech. The run-on line is more frequently used, and the placing of the caesura (a pause about the middle of a line) is more varied: 'Hell hath no limits nor is circumscrib'd/In one self place'.

Marlowe was a *dramatic poet* before he was a dramatist. He is weak in dialogue but strong in the set speeches. The most sustained dialogue in the play is between Faustus and Mephostophilis, though this tends to be a series of questions and answers, or speeches by Faustus that are near-soliloquies. It is here that Marlowe's greatness is demonstrated: Faustus's speeches are in a low key at the beginning of the play, but rise to a climax at the end. Marlowe's imagination, with its preoccupation with time, space and intellectual speculation, found ready and powerful expression in this kind of *rhetoric*.

Marlowe's poetic expression was often *lyrical*; this sometimes meant that it was static in stage terms. Such is the praise of Helen: its significance is in its beauty. It adds to the intellectual idea of the play but it does not result in stage action.

In intellectual terms the most notable lines in the play are statements. They do not necessarily proceed from the character of the speaker and they do not need a dramatic context, they stand absolutely and independently: 'Think'st thou heaven is such a glorious thing?/I tell thee, Faustus, it is not half so fair/As thou or any man that breathes on earth'. At its best the verse does not need external support; the final speech has in itself all the sense of movement, of urgency, of variety that is required. The verse has its own sense of climax: 'or let this hour be but/A year, a month, a week, a natural day'.

There is an abundant impression of action: 'Then will I headlong run into the earth./Earth, gape! O, no, it will not harbour me'. The imagery is violent but beautiful in its imaginative intensity: 'See, see where Christ's blood streams in the firmament!' The metre and line are varied to give dramatic emphasis: 'O God,/If thou wilt not have mercy on my soul . . . For when they die/Their souls are soon dissolv'd in elements'.

The speech to Helen is more lyrical but it has many of the same qualities. It opens on a question that is fittingly yet startlingly hyperbolic: 'Was this the face that launch'd a thousand ships/And burnt the topless towers of Ilium?' There is a breadth of *classical allusion* that seems to crowd the stage with heroes. Again, there is *hyperbole*, but also a true felicity, in 'O, thou art fairer than the evening's air/Clad in the beauty of a thousand stars'. But any address here is balanced by the warmth and richness of 'In wanton Arethusa's azur'd arms'. In these two passages the range and the certainty of the style reach the heights of great poetry; it is, of course, not always like this, and sometimes Marlowe fails to rise to the occasion. To compare the appearance of Helen to that of Alexander and his paramour is to place together two different worlds. Marlowe's choice of word is not the inevitable one.

His style, like his thought, is frequently one of *contrast and conflict*; the lines to Helen are recent enough in the play to be still in the memory of the audience as they listen to the final lines of Faustus; thus pointing the contrast between the ecstasy of love and the misery of a death that foreshadows the torture of eternal damnation. The contrasts are there throughout the play. The language expresses how Faustus is torn between the dogmas of the medieval world and the glories of the new world. The contrasts of extremes range everywhere: tragedy and farce; flippancy and seriousness; youth and age; hope and despair; heaven and hell; devils and angels; poetic imagination and the crudest of invention.

In some scenes the prose and verse lack all distinction. Marlowe was plainly happier with verse than with prose, and was at his best with serious and intense scenes and emotions.

It would be wrong to give the impression that Marlowe's style is only concerned with moments of great verse. He revelled also in pageantry. He may well have enjoyed the writing and presentation of 'shows' like *The Seven Deadly Sins*. He could introduce a dragon, which we know was one of the properties of the Lord Admiral's men. He was prepared to satisfy all the traditional demands of the contemporary audience. But that he was not slavishly dominated by these demands is shown by the transformation of the 'jigging veins' of his predecessors. The inequalities of his style and artistic approach are inevitable; judging historically, we should be astonished at what he did achieve, rather than condemn him for what he did not.

General questions and sample answer in note form

1 Describe the differences between Faustus's expectations of the powers that magic will bestow on him and the actual delight and power that magic is shown to bring.

2 The honesty of Mephostophilis is an admirable quality. Discuss.

3 In spite of his intellect, Faustus fails to understand the fact of his damnation. Discuss.

4 In tragedy the downfall of the hero is usually brought about by one major defect of character. Is this true of *Doctor Faustus*? If so, what is the defect?

5 The highest and noblest tragedy is here combined with contemptible and knockabout farce. Is this a fair judgement of *Doctor Faustus*?

6 Comment on the use of prose and verse in the play.

7 Faustus is a man caught between the modern and the medieval world. Discuss.

8 Describe the part played by the Chorus.

9 Give an account of the relationship between Faustus and Mephostophilis.

10 There is no real interplay of characters in *Doctor Faustus*; it is fundamentally a play about one man. Assess how far this is a weakness in the play.

11 Marlowe himself identifies with Faustus's intellectual zest and the consequent acceptance of damnation. How far is this true?

12 The moral purpose of the play is neither well stated nor well worked out. Discuss, stating what the moral purpose may be.

13 The claim to greatness lies in the poetry, not in the dramatic qualities. Discuss this judgement of *Doctor Faustus*.

14 To enjoy *Doctor Faustus* it is essential to accept the reality of the possibility of damnation. Consider how far this is true and to what extent Marlowe helps the audience in this acceptance.

15 Show how the conditions of the Elizabethan theatre and the nature of its audience influenced the construction and style of *Doctor Faustus*.

Suggested notes for essay answer to question 1

(a) *Introduction* – will summarise early part of play – easily seduced by the Evil Angel – promise of knowledge and power – potential to play God (which means rejection of God) – Mephostophilis.

(b) *The illusion of power over Mephostophilis* – all worldly power seems within his control – the bond which makes him yield up his soul after 24 years. First experiences the fact that Hell is real and not a fable – wants a wife but can't have one – power strictly limited by time and space.

(c) *Battle within his conscience* – influence of Good and Evil Angels – his yielding again despite moves towards repentance – descent into jokes and japes both low-life and high-life (the Pope) but without fulfilment. Displays skills and trickery but these are evanescent.

(d) *Triviality and the grotesque continue* – time manifestly wasted – despite the successful conjuration of Helen Faustus becomes convinced of his imminent damnation – riddled with conscience and fear – pleasures no longer pleasures but sins – repentance now impossible – too late.

(e) *Conclusion* – place some stress on structure – morality play – pace of action which overtakes Faustus – gratifications undermined by consciousness of evil and damnation.

Further reading

Critics on Marlowe: Readings in Literary Criticism, ed. Judith O'Neill (Allen and Unwin)
Marlowe, Doctor Faustus: A Casebook, ed. John D. Jump (Macmillan)
Christopher Marlowe: A Biography, A. L. Rowse (Macmillan)
Marlowe: A Critical Study, J. B. Stearne (OUP)